Competition in a Consolidating Environment

Zicklin School of Business Financial Markets Series

Robert A. Schwartz, Editor
Baruch College/CUNY
Zicklin School of Business
New York, NY, USA

Other Books in the Series:

Schwartz, Robert A., Byrne, John A., Colaninno, Antoinette:
The New NASDAQ Marketplace

Schwartz, Robert A., Byrne, John A., Colaninno, Antoinette:
Electronic vs. Floor Based Trading

Schwartz, Robert A., Byrne, John A., Colaninno, Antoinette:
Coping with Institutional Order Flow

Schwartz, Robert A., Byrne, John A., Colaninno, Antoinette:
A Trading Desk View of Market Quality

Schwartz, Robert A., Byrne, John A., Colaninno, Antoinette:
Call Auction Trading: New Answers to Old Questions

Schwartz, Robert A., Byrne, John A., Colaninno, Antoinette:
Regulation of U.S. Equity Markets

Robert A. Schwartz • John Aidan Byrne
Antoinette Colaninno
Editors

Competition in a Consolidating Environment

 Springer

Editors
Robert A. Schwartz
Zicklin School of Business
Baruch College, CUNY
One Bernard Baruch Way, B-10-225
New York NY 10010
robert_chwartz@baruch.cuny.edu

John Aidan Byrne

Antoinette Colaninno
Zicklin School of Business
Baruch College, CUNY
One Bernard Baruch Way, B-10-225
New York, NY 10010
antoinette_colaninno@baruch.cuny.edu

ISBN: 978-0-387-75942-5   e-ISBN: 978-0-387-75943-2
DOI: 10.1007/978-0-387-75943-2

Library of Congress Control Number: 2008935182

springer.com

Contents

Preface   vii

Conference Sponsors   xi

List of Participants   xiii

1   **Dialog with Reto Francioni**   1
    Reto Francioni and Robert A. Schwartz

2   **Global Winds of Change**   7
    Michael Pagano, Roland Bellegarde, Mark Guillaumier,
    Marcus Hooper, Susanne Kloess, Martin Reck, and Nic Stuchfield

3   **Intermarket Competition: Trading Decisions**   21
    Bob Pisani, Douglas Atkin, Michael Cormack, Alfred Eskandar,
    David Harris, and David Krell

4   **Intermarket Competition: Listing Decisions**   37
    Jamie Selway, Noreen Culhane, John Labuszewski,
    John McGonegal, and William O'Brien

5   **Emergence of New Competition: Alternative Sources of Liquidity** . . .   53
    William Harts, Alfred Berkeley, Luca Filippa, James Ross,
    George Sofianos, Larry Tabb, and Mark Wright

6   **The Countervailing Power of the Buy-Side**   69
    Michael Murphy, George Bodine, Paul Davis, Mark Forziati,
    Tim Mahoney, and Mony Rueven

7   **Dialog with Catherine Kinney**   89
    Catherine Kinney and Robert A. Schwartz

8   **Life After the Big Board Goes Electronic**   99
    Paul Davis, Michael S. Pagano, and Robert Schwartz

Participant Biographies. 111

Index 125

Preface

This book is an expanded account of *Competition in a Consolidating Environment*, a conference hosted on May 2, 2006, in the annual series by the Zicklin School of Business at Baruch College. The text includes the edited transcript of the full conference: five panels, as well as major presentations of two distinguished industry leaders – Reto Francioni, CEO, Deutsche Börse AG, and Catherine Kinney, President and Co-Chief Operating Officer of NYSE Euronext (back then called the NYSE Group).

Once again, this book, like the other popular books in the series, is more than an historical record. The manuscript has been heavily edited for clarity and unity of ideas. New material was included from interviews after the conference with many of the speakers. The intention has been to round out the panel discussions with more details while being careful not to sacrifice the essential nature of the original dialogue. The book also includes a related paper by Paul Davis, Mike Pagano, and myself: "Life After the Big Board Goes Electronic," *Financial Analysts Journal*, Volume 62, Number 5, September/October 2006, pp. 14–20.[1]

Throughout the editing process, John Byrne, Toni Colaninno, and I worked closely with the panelists to ensure that words were not put in their mouths. Extemporaneous comments are part of any lively panel, which add to the overall reading pleasure, sometimes as the result of careful editing. In any event, the panelists have all approved the final draft and we thank them for their assistance. We are also most grateful to our sponsors who made this conference possible (see page ix). Their funding and endorsement of our program are deeply appreciated.

I led off the conference with a statement I could have made in previous years. It seems to me that, with each passing year, the pace of change in our markets is accelerating. Our industry is experiencing change that is best described as seismic. The very landscape is being rattled by new technologies, new mergers, acquisitions and, of course, new regulations – Regulation NMS here in the U.S., and MiFID in Europe.

It is, indeed, wonderful to be living through and participating in this exciting period in Wall Street history. Even as markets are consolidating, new players are emerging. Just 2 weeks before this conference, the International Securities Exchange announced it was entering the equity space. What better demonstration than this of just how vibrant competition is? Fierce would be an even better word. But looking further down the road, if the dust ever finally settles on market structure, how consolidated will our markets be? How intense will competition remain?

When it comes to market structure regulation, the regulators like to focus on three areas: transparency, consolidation (or the inverse, fragmentation), and competition. Let us consider them for a moment. Electronic limit order platforms are inherently transparent vehicles. But we all know that big institutional investors simply will not send their big orders (either limit or market) to the book. If you have a trader doing that, look around in a week or two and you will see that he is a professor! The big investors slice and dice their orders. They use hidden orders (or iceberg orders as they are called in Europe). They send their orders to the more opaque upstairs market, or to an ATS which most likely is a dark liquidity pool.

The regulatory authorities may require that certain orders be exposed, but ultimately it is not possible in my opinion to legislate transparency. As I spoke those words at the conference, I was looking around (as I do in my evening classes) to see if the heads were moving vertically or horizontally. I saw quite a few vertical movements, and that was all that I needed to be encouraged.

With competition and consolidation, we have always been on the horns of a dilemma. That is because competition takes place in two ways that are antithetical to each other. There is competition within the order flow between different orders, and there is competition between different market centers. Competition within the order flow is most effective when orders are consolidated. I have always had my leanings in this direction. My bias has always been toward consolidation. My reason is that equity markets are networks; they enjoy something that we economists call "network externalities." What this means in plain English is that order flow attracts order flow. It means that, all else being equal, bigger markets are better markets. Bigger markets offer sharper price discovery, more liquidity, and better quantity discovery. They can do a better job of containing intraday volatility. As a network, an equity market is a natural monopoly.

There you have it, an economics professor talking positively about a monopoly. But, on the contrary, some fragmentation is called for because we want to have competition between the different trading vehicles. We depend on intermarket competition to keep exchange access fees reasonable, and to prevent markets suffering from technological inertia. Technological inertia has characterized our markets in the past. I do not know if it will ever do so again. So the question is, can we have our cake and eat it too? Can we let the order flow consolidate naturally through mergers and acquisitions, and still enjoy the benefits of vibrant competition? And what is the impact on competition of exchanges changing from membership organizations to for-profit organizations? Questions such as these need to be discussed, and this is what a conference such as this one here was all about.

Because of technology developments, the world of equity markets, in the words of Thomas Friedman, is flat. The enormous pressures for change that we are experiencing in the U.S. are not U.S. centric. They are felt around the globe. Europe currently has three major exchanges, London, Euronext, and Deutsche Börse. Each of the big three is well represented in our conference. What if the number of big exchanges in Europe were to shrink from three to two? What if one of them was to team up with a major U.S. market? In fact, after the conference, on April 4, 2007, the NYSE and Euronext merged to form one company, NYSE-Euronext. The first panel, which was moderated by my friend and long time coauthor, Mike Pagano, is titled Global Winds of Change. We learned more from that panel about the competitive scene from the perspective of France, Germany, England, Italy, the Far East, and Malta (a smaller exchange that is most enviably situated in the midst of a very large and sunny liquidity pool!). Also in the audience were a number of people from Canada, Germany, Spain, The Netherlands, and Australia. We very much appreciated their having traveled from afar to be with us.

Competition is not a simple concept. It is not monolithic. It exists in a number of ways and we should recognize this. In so doing, we might acquire more faith in the power of our markets to keep moving forward. Think of the phrase, running water purifies itself. In a similar fashion, competition can keep our markets pure. So, what are the sources of competition?

First, there is the competition that we all see and think about. Competition between the different trading centers and alternative trading vehicles. Competition of this type was discussed by the panel moderated by Bob Pisani, Intermarket Competition: Trading Decisions. Second, there is competition for the product that is traded (i.e., the listings). Competition of this type was addressed by the panel moderated by Jamie Selway, Intermarket Competition: Listing Decisions. Competition for the listings has been intense and vibrant. It is important to understand just how it will continue to play out in the future.

Bill Harts moderated the panel Emergence of New Competition: Alternative Sources of Liquidity. Technology opens new doors. Technology comes from and leads to new ideas and new ways of doing things. New players do enter the field even though it may be difficult for them to do so. Then there is one more source of competition that in recent years has truly arrived on the scene: the buy-side. The session headed by Mike Murphy was titled "The Countervailing Power of the Buy-Side." After crafting this title, I learned that some folks did not know the concept of countervailing power. It is an old Kenneth Galbraith term. When there is one big buyer, sellers pull together and fight back. When there is one big seller, buyers come together to counter the seller's power. It has taken the buy-side some time to do this. I remember not so many years ago when there were only a few people on the buy-side who stood out as a countervailing power. Mike Murphy was one of them, and he still is.

This is the seventh edited manuscript in Springer's Zicklin School of Business Financial Markets Series. Over the years, as our topics evolve and our conferences proceed, it is fascinating to look back and see how our thoughts have changed and our focus has altered. A lot of thought-provoking ideas were exchanged and much was said during the May 2, 2006, conference. That discussion makes an excellent seventh addition to the conference series.

Robert A. Schwartz

Conference Sponsors

American Stock Exchange
Banc of America Securities
BNY Brokerage
Deutsche Börse AG
Edge Trade Inc.
Financial News
International Capital Market Association
International Securities Exchange
ITG, Inc.
Knight Capital Group, Inc.
Liquidnet, Inc.
NYSE Euronext
Pipeline Trading Systems
The Nasdaq Stock Market, Inc.
White Cap Trading, LLC

List of Participants

Brooke Allen   Maple Securities   Head, Quantitative Trading
*At the time of the conference, Mr. Allen was with MANE Fund Management, Inc.

Douglas Atkin   Majestic Research   President & CEO

Stephen Balog   Cedar Creek Management   Managing Partner

Roland Bellegarde   Euronext NV   Deputy CEO, Euronext Cash Market

Alfred Berkeley   Pipeline Trading Systems   Chairman & CEO

George Bodine   General Motors Investment Management   Director of Trading

Don Calvin*   International Business Enterprises   Chairman
*At the time of the conference, Mr. Calvin was Chairman of the National Stock Exchange.

Isabelle Clary*   Pensions & Investments   Reporter
*At the time of the conference, Ms. Clary was a Reporter with Financial News.

Michael Cormack*
*At the time of the conference, Mr. Cormack was Executive Vice President at the NYSE Group, Inc.

Noreen Culhane   NYSE Euronext   Executive Vice President

Paul Davis   TIAA-CREF Investment Management LLC   Retired Managing Director

Alfred Eskandar   Liquidnet, Inc.   Director of Corporate Strategy

Eric Exner   Accenture   Senior Manager

Luca Filippa   Borsa Italiana   Director, Research & Development

Shane Finemore   UBS Securities LLC   Managing Director

Anthony Fortunato*	Instinet, LLC	Head of Sales, New England

*At the time of the conference, Mr. Fortunato was Director of U.S. Equity Sales and Trading at Nomura Securities International.

Mark Forziati	Tudor Investment Corporation	Senior Vice President
Reto Francioni	Deutsche Börse AG	CEO
William Freund	Pace University	Professor
Marc Gresack	MatchPoint Trading	President
Mark Guillaumier	Malta Stock Exchange	Chief Executive Officer
David Harris*	CBOE Stock Exchange	CEO

*At the time of the conference, Mr. Harris was Senior Vice President at the American Stock Exchange.

William Harts	Banc of America Securities	Managing Director
Marcus Hooper	Duvacy Ltd.	
Brian Hyndman	The Nasdaq Stock Market, Inc.	Senior Vice President
Catherine Kinney	NYSE Euronext	President and Co-Chief Operating Officer
Susanne Kloess	Accenture	Managing Director
David Krell	International Securities Exchange	President & CEO
John Labuszewski	Chicago Mercantile Exchange	Managing Director
Tim Mahoney*	Bids Trading	

*At the time of the conference, Mr. Mahoney was Head of Equity Trading at Merrill Lynch Investment Management.

John McGonegal*

*At the time of the conference, Mr. McGonegal was Senior Vice President at the American Stock Exchange.

Michael Murphy	Piney Run Capital LLC	Founder and President
William O'Brien	The Nasdaq Stock Market, Inc.	Senior Vice President
Michael Pagano	Villanova University	Associate Professor of Finance

Bob Pisani	CNBC	Correspondent
Martin Reck	Deutsche Börse AG	Managing Director
James Ross*	NYSE Euronext	VP, NYSE Crossing

*At the time of the conference, Mr. Ross was CEO of MatchPoint Trading.

Mony Rueven	D.E. Shaw & Co.	Managing Director
Stephen Sax	Floor Broker Network	Vice President
Jamie Selway	White Cap Trading, LLC	Chairman & Managing Director
George Sofianos	Goldman Sachs	Vice President
Nic Stuchfield	London Stock Exchange	Director of Corporate Development
Larry Tabb	The Tabb Group	Founder & CEO
Bob Wood	University of Memphis	Professor
Mark Wright	ITG, Inc.	Managing Director

Chapter 1
Dialog with Reto Francioni

Reto Francioni and Robert A. Schwartz

ROBERT SCHWARTZ: I have known Reto Francioni and have worked with him over the years. He is a good friend. I very much appreciate his having traveled from Frankfurt to be with us today. That said, I will now ask him some questions that are designed to make him feel uncomfortable (laughter).

Let us start at the beginning. What in your opinion are the key drivers of consolidation? Why all of a sudden are we hearing all these merger talks that involve Deutsche Börse, Euronext and the London Stock Exchange?

RETO FRANCIONI: The first key element is that all three of these major exchange organizations are listed. This simple fact is a necessary pre-condition for these mergers. In Europe and elsewhere, a stock exchange is not just a stock exchange anymore. It is also a public company. Listed stock exchanges have many constituencies: there is the legislative government, regulatory authorities, customers, shareholders, and the very proud management running the companies. As you can imagine, it is not easy to get all of these constituencies together.

The second key element is ownership. There have been a lot of changes in this area. These companies are owned by foreign investors now. For instance, 90% of Deutsche Börse is owned by foreign shareholders. This has very much affected the framework of our corporate governance.

The third key element is a regulatory environment that has changed and is still changing. Bob mentioned the Markets in Financial Instruments Directive or MiFID. MiFID is a European directive in the secondary market area. It focuses on internalization and netting.

A fourth component will be familiar in the U.S. As I have mentioned, the big U.S. stock exchanges are now listed. On a strategic level, they have the information technology needed to become international. Here in New York and also in Chicago, very important events have occurred that have had quite an impact on the European scene.

To answer your question, these four elements, which have come into place, have triggered the recent developments in Europe.

SCHWARTZ: In assessing a merger, would you put more weight on cost saving, on market quality, or on revenue generation?

FRANCIONI: You have just two sides of the P&L. There is the cost side and the income side. A merger is of necessity about costs, but that alone is not sufficient.

R.A. Schwartz et al. (eds.), *Competition in a Consolidating Environment*,
doi: 10.1007/978-0-387-75943-2_1, © Springer Science+Business Media, LLC 2008

When two organizations come together, the merger should have an impact on the income side as well. A merger will impact the income side by producing a better distribution of power, by enabling a more attractive product range with which to formulate other strategies, and so on. For instance, the talks between Euronext and Deutsche Börse also include the derivative markets. So, additional assets can be created when you are combined.

SCHWARTZ: This might be a complicated question to answer: do you think that MiFID, when it gets instituted, will be a force for consolidation, or not?

FRANCIONI: Bob, it depends (laughter).

SCHWARTZ: Some of you might remember that "it depends" was a popular refrain at one of our conferences a couple of years ago (laughter).

FRANCIONI: To specify the factors in a little more detail, MiFID is not just a sort of European trade-through rule. It also affects the possibility for internalizing.[1] The value chain includes investors, intermediaries, the stock exchange, clearing and settlement, and then back to the intermediaries. The possibility is created through MiFID that the intermediaries (the last part of the value chain before price discovery occurs) can do a kind of netting. They can net customer buy and sell orders and go to the exchange with just the difference. One could be scared of this because less volume will be brought to the stock exchange, which could harm the quality of price discovery.

On the other hand, in Germany there never was a rule to direct your flows to the stock exchange. Therefore, internalization is nothing new for the German market as we have already had to cope with it for years. We are even operating a platform – Xetra Best – for intermediaries, to support their internalization services on a technical basis.

To summarize, for Deutsche Börse as a stock exchange organization, MiFID is not a threat but a chance for growth. We will very carefully watch what the intermediaries do. In order to do this kind of internalization (netting), you must have huge flows, so the intermediaries who do this tend to be big players, and they do so in very liquid stocks. Netting is not a risk-free business. To do it correctly requires

---

[1] MiFID, the Markets in Financial Instruments Directive for securities trading in Europe, is an EU directive that replaces the Investment Services Directive. MiFID aims to make cross-border trading in Europe simpler, fairer and cheaper for financial institutions and investors by promoting competition between trading venues and mandating pre- and post-trade transparency. MiFID in Europe and Reg NMS in the U.S. have some similarities in the area of best execution. However, the Reg NMS trade-through rule is not as flexible as the MiFID approach on best execution. Unlike Reg NMS, MiFID permits other factors that could influence best execution, including transaction cost, speed and the expectations for execution and settlement. Analysts note that although MiFID is a more acceptable approach to trading participants, the downside is enforcement. "When a best execution is determined on the basis of price, it is easier to detect whether or not the requirements have been fulfilled than when a whole area of variables can satisfy best execution requirements, based on the clients preference," according to Jean-Pierre Carey and Karen Lanno. (See, European Capital Markets Institute (ECMI) Policy Brief, No. 1, May 2006.)

detailed analysis, and this requires very expensive IT systems. Therefore, you must invest a lot of money to make it run profitably.

SCHWARTZ: To what extent is netting and internalization facilitated by the quality of the job that you do at the exchange? It seems to me that it is a lot easier to make trades that customers will be satisfied with away from the exchange if they can be made at good prices. And, the prices are produced on the exchange. So it gets into the issue of free riding. Do you think of it in this way?

FRANCIONI: Yes. The stock exchange price will always be used as a reference point for the netting. You cannot do netting out of the blue. That is a challenge for those who are doing it because of exposure to volatility risk on the book of the netting intermediary.

SCHWARTZ: Because I am an economist, when I use the term "free-riding," it sounds like something that is not good. Yet it is part of the reality of the industry. What I find interesting about it is that the better the job that you do, the more people will free ride on the job that you do. There seems to be a natural amount of fragmentation away from the exchange. But does this not imply competition, our topic here today? The exchange market is competing with the off-board, upstairs market.

FRANCIONI: Yes. And that was always the case. That will always be the case, and it is not the worst thing.

SCHWARTZ: It is a good thing to note the existence of this competition if you are worried about a regulator saying that you have too much market share. Free riding and off-board trading appear to be a natural, self-sustaining force for competition.

FRANCIONI: We do not see it as too much market share. All the liquidity a stock exchange has is used to provide the best possible price. This is also assured by the system. You can see price discovery with our market structure. Our order book is open and very transparent. You see what you get, and you get what you see. The more orders we receive, the better is the quality of the price discovery that we deliver.

SCHWARTZ: I always like to call attention to price discovery. I think it is an under-recognized function of an exchange. We recognize it to some extent, but a lot of discussions pay insufficient attention to it.

FRANCIONI: It is our main function. In the very end, price discovery is the number one product that we deliver.

SCHWARTZ: You produce the price.

FRANCIONI: Yes.

SCHWARTZ: I would like to ask another question. I am interested in Thomas Friedman's thought that the world is flat. In some respects the world is flat, and in other respects the world is not. Could you comment, Reto, in this context, about combining or consolidating markets? What about the possibility of a trans-Atlantic partnership with a U.S., European combination? This is a simple question, no?

FRANCIONI: Yes, the question is simple, but my answer to it is not. To put it bluntly, there are a lot of possibilities. But in the very end, there will be two partners, one from each side. They will have to present a strong pitch that it makes sense to get together, that by combining they will be able to create more than they could by standing alone. The opportunity must be there to create a customized, tailor-made package with a range of challenges and opportunities to go overseas.

SCHWARTZ: With the seismic changes that are occurring in the industry, it is a bit hard to see how the pieces will come together. Are there any questions from the audience?

STEVE BALOG (Cedar Creek Management) [From the Floor]: Could you help me to understand the cost synergies as you see them, if any, in a U.S.-European exchange merger? I would think that they are not as obvious as when a NASDAQ and an INET get together. I have been struggling with this for some time. You have to keep two software systems, two data centers, maybe two regulatory departments, because they do not fit together as well as an entity within one country. I have been baffled as to what the great cost synergies are of a trans-Atlantic merger.

FRANCIONI: There is no general rule or statement about this. You have to take a close look at what is at stake. When you have two different systems, you keep one and write off the other. You have to deal with questions such as, what is best for our customers? What does the user think about these changes? Will the switching costs affect the quality of service that you deliver to the customer? Then there is the pure cost side within this merged entity. Perhaps the more expensive system has lower switching costs[2] and higher service quality. It is very difficult to discuss this in general terms.

In the very end, you have to make management decisions about what you are going to cut, what you are going to switch. This has to be implemented in a common IT strategy. You cannot just calculate the cut because it has to be considered over a period of time, perhaps one, or two, or even three years. It is a key analysis that has to be done on several premises, plus on a mid-term basis. It is difficult to be more specific than that if we are not looking at a concrete case. This is a general, in your case probably unsatisfactory, answer to your concrete question.

SCHWARTZ: More questions?

PAUL DAVIS (TIAA-CREF) [From the Floor]: Thinking about the competition that exists between exchanges and the major brokerage firms who internalize much order flow, the exchanges have brokers who are their customers. In light of this competition between exchanges and brokers, is the Deutsche Börse thinking of going to the large institutions and creating a product that goes directly to them?[3]

---

[2] Reto Francioni is referring, hypothetically, to the "switching" costs of adapting a more expensive IT system over another in the merged entity. He posits that using the more expensive system could potentially drive down overall operational costs and improve performance.

[3] Davis is referring to Deutsche Börse offering its services to institutional customers, bypassing its brokerage customers for order flow directly from the buy-side.

FRANCIONI: To do this, you have to analyze in more detail the legal or regulatory framework. Within Eurex, you could do it now. There is no legal obstacle to a big institution having direct access to the price discovery feature, which means the stock exchange, and therefore becoming a kind of intermediary in legal terms. Having the option to choose the broker or the intermediary is of value to a big player. When it comes to execution topics (speed of execution and so forth), this is an asset for the big player. He or she can use different tactics to execute different orders. So, this is the question: is there a need to do so? For us, it is not a question of approaching the buy-side directly. We will hold on to our intermediary structure, which is given by law. If such a company in the derivative markets wants to take part they can do so. It is a different story in the cash markets because they have to fulfill different criteria. There are different levels of being an intermediary or a member at the stock exchange. Nevertheless, we do not intend to break the legally defined intermediary structure.

SCHWARTZ: One more question?

DEIGO PERFUMO (Efficient Frontiers) [From the Floor]: Reto, you mentioned competing with the OTC markets. Eurex is planning to bring new products that are currently trading OTC, for example SpotFX, into your own exchange. Could you comment on this?

FRANCIONI: We are planning several new products in the derivatives area. As you can imagine, I cannot talk about these products before they are launched. But I can say that we do have plans for new products.

SCHWARTZ: Let me end with the final question. Will you come back next year and answer more questions?

FRANCIONI: It depends, Bob, but yes (laughter).

Chapter 2
Global Winds of Change

Michael Pagano, Roland Bellegarde, Mark Guillaumier, Marcus Hooper, Susanne Kloess, Martin Reck, and Nic Stuchfield

MICHAEL PAGANO: We have a very distinguished set of speakers on this panel. I will start things off with a few questions but, as Bob always says, please feel free to ask us questions from the floor at any time.

The title of the panel is the Global Winds of Change. I will start with Martin Reck. Martin, given the panel's title, would you say that the winds buffeting today's global equity markets are a summer breeze, a hurricane, or something in between? What specifically is driving these winds?

MARTIN RECK: Mike, I learned to sail when I was a boy. It is always good to have wind. If your boat is in good shape and you have a good crew, let the wind come. There is nothing bad about that. To continue with your analogy, today the wind is increasing. We have to focus on the factors that are triggering that increase. Today, market consolidation is the name of the game. That has been the case during the last 18–24 months. The new thing is that it is now happening across different time zones. It is also hitting different areas of our industry. Not just the exchanges, but the intermediaries and investors as well. One thing that has triggered these changes was (on our side of the Atlantic at least) a dramatic volume increase in certain instruments.

For instance, in the Eurex derivatives market we had 1.3 billion contracts in 2005. That is a 20% increase over 2004. Since we introduced the market maker program in our equity options in 2005, we have had a tenfold increase in the number of quotes coming in from market makers. That is a massive volume increase. Then you see innovation. Someone asked about new products and services on our side. Yes, we focus on our product development on the on-exchange as well as on the off-exchange segments.

Clearing is an interesting field. We have to consider what innovations we as an exchange, or a clearinghouse, can bring to the market, in particular to part of the OTC market. Then there is regulation. We mentioned MiFID earlier. MiFID, to a certain extent, will reshape the power game among European exchanges, trading venues and intermediaries. We have to be aware of employing technology. Our customers are just as innovative in applying technology as we are. All of my colleagues here are facing algorithmic trading, and we have to serve algorithmic traders. We are preparing to ramp up our systems to cope with that. We are further preparing to go with that trend and are offering good service to our company. These are the big factors that have triggered change.

R.A. Schwartz et al. (eds.), *Competition in a Consolidating Environment*,
doi: 10.1007/978-0-387-75943-2_2, © Springer Science+Business Media, LLC 2008

PAGANO: Other comments?

NIC STUCHFIELD: One of the major realities driving change is that historically exchange companies have been very cheap. In the beginning of the twenty-first century, in the early days of the exchange IPOs, the market did not appreciate the value of exchanges. Indeed, some of our suitors failed to appreciate the value of our assets as well (laughter). My company was described as being a boring utility. We have, as Martin has said, experienced significant growth. A lot of that has been due to the fact that algorithmic trading has greatly reduced the cost of intermediation, which has favored the exchanges. Algorithmic trading makes it a lot more efficient for investment bankers to break orders up and to run them through the exchanges' order books.

A number of us, certainly the London Exchange, have invested significantly in technology to reduce latency and to increase capacity in order to facilitate this greater volume. We have seen a sort of "hurry up and buy these assets while they are cheap" phenomenon. Now exchanges are not so cheap, and it remains to be seen what will happen.

Competing with exchanges is not easy because of the network externalities that Bob Schwartz referred to earlier. We are in an environment where it is probably (but not necessarily, certainly) easier to consolidate than to compete.

PAGANO: Are you saying that this is making better sailing for everyone? That you are both more valuable and faster?

STUCHFIELD: We probably have the purest market in corporate control at the London Stock Exchange. This is because we probably are the least nationalistic and have the least regulatory defenses of all major exchanges in the world. We have never complained about this. We enjoy the discipline that this forces upon us. It forces us to get better and to be better at doing what we do. In the nicest possible way, we continue to drive our service quality forward so that we can be maximally attractive to the investment banking community and their customers. We want to ensure that people choose to do their business on our order book rather than internalize it.

PAGANO: Susanne, where is the growth potential? Is it coming from consolidating North American or Western European exchanges, or do you see things happening in Asia or developing countries where there may be even greater synergies or growth potential?

SUSANNE KLOESS: To repeat a very famous phrase, it depends (laughter). We will, I am sure, continue to hear that phrase several more times throughout today. When I look at it from a distance, you can actually have growth from various sources. If you look at highly developed markets (like the U.S. and the European markets), you can still have growth here. You heard from Nic and Martin that they both are facing a lot of growth in terms of order volume and transaction volume. If you want to deal with that kind of growth and still make a lot of money (which, as a matter of fact, listed exchanges are looking to do), then you must optimize your operations and your IT costs. A lot of growth will definitely result if you do that well. It is a totally different story for emerging markets.

Looking at Central/Eastern Europe, Latin America, and Asia (mainly China and India), these are all countries that may not be on our radar screen just now. However, if I could look into a crystal ball, I would think that, in the next 5–10 years, these regions will be growing and taking over positions that we could not think of them having today. They can grow because their markets are not yet fully developed. They are just starting. They have a growth journey ahead that the fully developed markets in Europe and North America have behind them. They are in a different phase. The growth will come from building these markets up, which is a different type of growth.

Let me share one example with you. On Mainland China, there is a stock exchange in Shanghai that is building a new, next generation trading system. They are facing 80 million accounts that they need to support with their IT system. If you can imagine that many people trading, both through intermediaries and directly – direct access is allowed there by law – you are definitely facing a different growth scenario.

Take Japan as another example. They are trying to attract outside listings. We will see a lot of growth coming out of that. It is a business that we often forget to talk about. I can see growth coming out of the listing business in Europe as well. The Tokyo Stock Exchange is ready to list 10 or more Chinese companies right now. They made that public. That will definitely give Tokyo another angle of competition, and a place for growth.

PAGANO: Marcus?

MARCUS HOOPER: I would like to pick up on several threads that have been mentioned so far. One of the questions that Bob Schwartz asked earlier is about consolidation and MiFID. I agree, it does depend. There is no question about that. But if you think of MiFID as a very broad ranging force in the industry – which it is – you have to ask whether everyone within those jurisdictions is prepared for it.

When you take a closer look, there are an awful lot of people who are not prepared, people who have not really been engaged very much. If that remains the case, consolidation will more likely occur. Those firms that simply cannot meet the regulatory requirements will have to adapt, or else effectively sell themselves because there will be no alternative.

I have had quite a lot of experience trading. I agree with Nic's comments earlier about efficiency and the use of algorithms. But that is actually a symptom of the markets at the moment. That is not necessarily what I, as a trader, would think of as efficiency. It is a mechanized way of doing something that is quite inefficient, namely, slicing up order flow into very small pieces so that you can get your order done without exposing it to gaming, and to information disclosure. That is what you are trying to achieve.

But there is another game in town, and that is to reconcile block trading. I had a conversation with someone at an exchange before coming in here. We were discussing exactly that issue: can you ever reconcile this issue of block trading and meet the information disclosure requirement? Personally, I think that there are ways to do it and that we will see some very innovative approaches in the future. We have seen some interesting ATSs, but the question is, how do you strike that right balance?

MiFID will promote increased transparency. You will have trading participants sharing more trade data across the various European markets in the trade clearance and settlement process. The retail and wholesale, or institutional markets, will have more equal standing, as the idea is to encourage fairer markets, and a common European standard of best execution. There has to be some linkage between these two markets. That is an area where we will see some significant product development in the future. Go back to the wind analogy. This is one of those very very hot tropical winds where you are sitting on the beach, you got there at 9 o'clock in the morning, it gets hotter, and it gets hotter, and it gets hotter. The question is, at lunchtime, how many people are still on the beach and how many are in the bar (laughter)?

PAGANO: Mark, from your perspective in Malta, could you add to some of the things that Susanne and Martin spoke about?

MARK GUILLAUMIER: The Malta Stock Exchange is a much smaller entity than the London Stock Exchange or Deutsche Börse. Malta has a population of 400,000 and the local stock exchange has been around for 14 years, since 1992. In 2004, Malta became part of the European Union, which means that we are faced with the same kind of directives and regulations as London and Germany. Basically, it is a question of survival for emerging markets and for smaller stock exchanges. The objective of MiFID is to increase the level of competition. What has been happening? Around Europe, we have seen a lot of markets merging or consolidating. The Baltic States are now part of the OMX,[1] and Cyprus is becoming part of the Athens set up. We are looking at revising our strategy. We are streamlining our operations and cutting our costs, increasing the level of our services, etc. As a smaller stock exchange, we have to try and be more competitive. We need more distribution into the U.S. As Bob Schwartz has said, we are also sitting on a pool of liquidity. Malta is part of the Mediterranean region. We are on the border of the Middle East and the South of the Gulf. We have been doing some work in that direction. What do I see in my crystal ball? An exciting road ahead.

PAGANO: Do you think that investing in IT would be a way to plug into that world out there?

GUILLAUMIER: Our operations are completely IT based – technologically updated if you like. Yes, we are investing heavily in IT. We believe that this is one way to streamline operations, to cut down on costs, and to get better connectivity with the main markets of Europe.

PAGANO: Roland, I was thinking about this from the perspective of national regulators. Now you have all these publicly traded companies out there, you have the managements having agendas, and also activist shareholders. How do the national regulators fit into this equation?

ROLAND BELLEGARDE: The regulators have a role to play in regulating the exchanges and the markets, as they have done for the past few years. Exchanges are not normal companies. They are running financial markets, and those markets are places where capital is provided for companies. The exchanges were previously monopolies. Now they are listed. But they have very specific ways of doing

---

[1] OMX AB, the Swiss-Finnish financial services company established in 2003 from a merger between OM AB and HEX Plc., has two units, OMX Exchanges and OMX Technology.

business, and you have to be very close to their businesses to understand their operations. There can be a potential for mismanagement of markets. That is why we have strong relationships with the five regulators of Euronext.

This is quite unique, having five regulators getting together to produce a common rulebook for our markets. The regulators have a role to play in monitoring the markets, especially with regard to exchanges, although the shareholders have their own say about their future.

PAGANO: The five regulators you mentioned, who is the fifth? You have four markets (Paris, Amsterdam, Brussels and Lisbon), so I assume that you have four national regulators.

BELLEGARDE: Plus LIFFE in London. We have four cash markets and five derivatives markets. That is why we have five regulators from the five Euronext countries. They meet on a regular basis. We submit a set of rules to them, they commonly agree on this set of rules, and they then reflect those rules in their national regulations. This is how we get common, harmonized rules for the exchanges, for the cash on one side, and for the derivatives on the other. We have a common set of rules, a common platform, and a common framework, even though we have five exchanges, four countries, plus one more country on the derivatives side. It is a unique example of how we can get to common, efficient rules, supported by one single trading platform and one single clearing entity.

PAGANO: When it comes to global or international cross-border mergers, could that model potentially play out? Let's just take a wild example, how about NASDAQ and the LSE (laughter). How would that play out in your view Roland? And in your view also, Nic? I am sure that you both have some thoughts on this as well.

STUCHFIELD: I do. It is worth first pointing out something that may not be obvious to a largely American audience – MiFID will not actually create a single pan-European capital market. It may or may not have been designed to do that, but it certainly will not succeed in doing that. I would be interested if my colleagues here on the panel would agree with that.

Euronext has made the best of the relatively messy political and regulatory environment that existed in Europe post the original Investment Services Directive. That messy environment will not substantially change as a result of MiFID. Countries still regard having a national stock exchange as a badge of pride. The ability to take the exchanges of multiple countries and turn them into a single exchange is very constrained. Euronext has made the best of this difficult situation by doing the best that you can do, short of collapsing the exchange structures into one another.

The issue of a European–U.S. exchange, generally speaking, would be very similar. I do not think that the U.S. Securities and Exchange Commission would be very keen on having one of the two major U.S. markets operated out of Europe. I do not think that any of the national regulators in Europe – the FSA certainly – would be very keen on having a U.K. market (or the regulator in any other European jurisdiction, which tend to be less open) being run from America. So what are the benefits of a trans-Atlantic merger? We heard some questioning by Reto Francioni on this earlier. My own view is that it is possible to slim down to a singular piece of software. Increasingly, market structures are becoming more closely aligned. We operate a hybrid market, the NYSE is moving toward a hybrid market, and NASDAQ is a hybrid market in a very real sense. At the same time, technology is becoming more flexible, and it will be able to accommodate the little bells and whistles that inevitably exist between countries that have different ways of doing business.

Within Europe you could probably consolidate the number of data centers, but that will not be possible in the short term across the Atlantic. This is because the latency involved in getting data across the Atlantic does not support the real-time need of trading that is increasingly being measured in milliseconds.[2] There are some economies that one could realize in a transatlantic merger. They are probably less than could be realized from an intra-European merger. But in either case I do not think that it is possible to consider the creation of a single pan-European, or for that matter a global, capital market. This is something that many of us, and certainly the academicians among us, would consider the long-term objective of consolidation.

BELLEGARDE: I do not think that your statement on the regulators is correct, or the fact that we cannot reach harmonized or unified markets in Europe with MiFID. To think of just waiting until we have one single regulator – and that everything would then be harmonized by the other entities and authorities – is not acceptable. Obviously we would have to wait a very long time for that.

When we began Euronext we said, OK, we will face the fact that we do not have a single regulator. We will embark on getting to one harmonized rulebook supported by one single platform. This showed our determination to get one single market platform, and we wanted the approval of all the regulators to try to achieve it. Obviously it is not easy, but you cannot wait for it. You must embark on a difficult path to get to that point. MiFID is just allowing more competition, allowing more freedom for market players. It will not create a single market. But it will create the right framework to try to get to that point. Someone has to do it.

---

[2] As Stuchfield mentioned earlier, the London Stock Exchange, responding to customer demand for speedier order executions, invested heavily in technology aimed at reducing system latency. These customers react almost instantaneously, by computerized trading, to potentially market-moving information, so low latency is a critical factor. Indeed, many of these customers need to react and route orders at a rate that some analysts equate with the speed of light. By the same token, in any merger of two exchanges on separate continents (in this instance, North America and Europe), as Stuchfield elaborated in an interview after the conference, there is "an unavoidable requirement" at this time to maintain primary data centers in each of the continents. For some trading customers in these fast markets, "sub-10 millisecond latency is important," as Stuchfield observed. Stuchfield noted that light travels at some 186,000 miles per second (mps), so he calculated that it would take about 20 milliseconds (ms) for light to travel the roughly 3,500 miles between the trading markets of London and New York without any electronic routers or other delays in the way. (Divide 3,500 by 186,000 to arrive at approximately 20 ms. A millisecond is one thousandth of a second.) But this 20 ms "delay," calculated at the speed of light, was still too long a time for traders who use strategies that engage rapid-fire trading across the span of continents. Clearly, primary data centers were still required in each of the continents.

STUCHFIELD: I do not think that we disagree. I was actually trying to be compli-mentary to you in my earlier comment. The European Commission desires to have a single financial market, but the framework of legislation that it has put in place will not, in my opinion, deliver that. I think I heard you agree with that towards the end of your comment, Roland.

BELLEGARDE: Yes, it will not create that framework. It will not create one single entity for trading, one single entity for clearing, and one single entity for settlement. But it will create conditions for the competition that will get us to that point. If no one is trying to get the benefit of this new framework, if no one is trying to get to this point, then obviously we will not have one single market in Europe.

RECK: MiFID will make things clearer in Europe. The regulation tells you in terms of transparency reporting what you must do if you are an exchange, if you are a trading venue, and if you are an internalizer. That is important in our land-scape because the practices are still very different. Take the consolidation rule in France (which under MiFID will go away), or the reporting requirements in London (the game will change for them). These developments open up the field for other players. As an exchange, you must consider what MiFID is and how you react to it.

Whether you are ready or not, we believe that we are ready and quite well pre-pared. You have to look into new fields of business that might open up. So help your customers get prepared for MiFID. Help them to fulfill their obligations.

STUCHFIELD: Indeed we are doing just that. We regard MiFID as an opportunity rather than as a threat. For the longest time trading participants have had the com-plete liberty to internalize orders and just trade report them. As a consequence, that part of our business contributes only very modestly to our top line. The same set of rules will now be applied throughout the E.U. countries. They will bring clarity to the opportunity for investment firms to become systematic internalizers, or multi-lateral trading systems. We expect some new firms to arise. This certainly opens an opportunity for increased competition.

Nevertheless, the network externalities that the order books of the major exchanges offer are very powerful factors. This implies that most of that competi-tion will be in what we call the off-book space. This trading usually takes place bilaterally, between brokers and banks, or via internalization by two clients dealing with the same bank, for example. Therefore, the competition is in the trade report-ing space, rather than in the order -book space of the public limit order books of the various markets, such as SETS, Xetra, INET etc. So this is the principle economic driver of all of our top lines. The regulators require off-book trades to be reported for regulatory and transparency reasons. In the U.S. and U.K., at least, banks and financial firms can report trades to a number of venues. In a post-MiFID environ-ment, however, they will also be able to do so in the rest of the European Union, thus generating this competition in the off-book space.

RECK: It will be interesting to see how trading venues explain best execution when you trade outside the exchange. How can they explain to their customers how they guarantee best execution? It will be interesting to see how this develops.

BELLEGARDE: As Marcus mentioned, the new potential will come out in how blocks are traded. This is basically where you can develop a niche market. That is because competing with order books that are very efficient for mid-size trades, I have to admit, is something that is probably much more difficult. I expect that we will face more competition from the block trading facilities and crossing networks.

PAGANO: You all seem to be saying that MiFID's coming is an opportunity rather than a threat. In terms of order consolidation or fragmentation, what do you think will be happening in your part of the world as you deal with MiFID? Will it fragment the market, or will it create better opportunities for consolidation amongst those who are more efficient? Perhaps someone in the audience would like to join in on this?

DON CALVIN (International Business Enterprises)[3] [From the floor]: I was involved in the New York Stock Exchange back in the 1970s when Congress was hell bent on creating something that they called a National Market System. Much of this discussion today resembles what we heard back then. The point was made then – successfully, I might add – that the competition that is important is the competition among orders in setting the prices. Not competition among organizations to do whatever they would do. What came out of that was the Intermarket Trading System that is linking markets so that you could have competition among orders. My question is, has there been much discussion in Europe about the possible linking of the markets as was done here?

BELLEGARDE: The difference between Europe and the U.S. is that in Europe we cannot compete only on the execution prices because we do not have a single post-trade infrastructure. Clearing and settlement is not standardized as in the U.S. You cannot compare or define best execution on the execution price alone. Thus, you cannot create an inter-linkage between the markets to route orders. That is why best execution is particularly vague in the European directive. This leaves the market professionals in front of the difficulties to define what best execution is. They have defined their policy and explained it to their customers. It will encompass more than just the execution price. It will include all other elements, including clearing and settlement and brokerage costs.

RECK: We should also recognize that in Europe we do not have an overlap between the lists of stocks that are traded on different exchanges. We still have this home market concentration. Consequently, an inter-market trading system through which you could arbitrage or organize liquidity between the same stock in different order books is not so pressing.

HOOPER: Your question is extremely perceptive. The reason is that, at the moment, exchanges are still thinking of this consolidating environment as simply being about takeovers and mergers. If you go to any trading desk where data is fragmented in Europe, you will find that, as the technology improves, this consolidation

---

[3] At the time of the conference, Mr. Calvin was Chairman of the National Stock Exchange.

of information is being done locally anyway, or else is being provided by a market data vendor, such as Reuters, or an aggregator. One of the intentions of MiFID is to create a common approach to data availability that it will allow competition to occur more freely. [4] An example that was mentioned earlier is implicit in the question, where is the right price? Let's take an ECN or an ATS of some kind that creates a large order through its multi-lateral trading facility. Let two contras trade stock at 250 when the exchange price is 240. If the ATS has actually done a massive block of stock versus a tiny amount on the exchange, who is to say that the block trader is incorrect?

PAGANO: Yes, that points something out. What are customers in Europe asking your exchanges? They are talking to all of you piecemeal, but collectively they must be wondering, for example, if there is a demand for trading London Stocks at the same venue as Parisian stocks? Are you getting that kind of interest from your customers?

STUCHFIELD: The investment banks have lived in an environment with multiple exchanges. They have adjusted to that environment technologically. They have highly integrated systems that enable complex, multi-national orders, switches between stocks in one country and stocks in another, and so forth. Orders can be broken up and handled in a very effective and seamless way across different exchange environments. In a sense, the investment banking community, having bridged across the exchanges, has facilitated the single European capital market. The demand for it is a function of the ultimate investor, and whether or not he or she wants to buy a predominantly U.K. portfolio, or a predominantly German portfolio or, for that matter, a pan-European portfolio.

We do extensive customer research and customer relations management both with our sell-side customers and with their customers, the buy-side. What tends to be requested of us are the things that you would expect – faster and cheaper execution, more liquidity, greater transparency, complete fairness, and the essential trusted nature of being a stock exchange. Trust is something that is never to be compromised. Those are the kinds of things that we try to achieve in our strategic management policies – reducing the cost of our technology to our customers, increasing the level of liquidity, reducing spreads, maintaining trust, and so on.

PAGANO: As you do these things, are you primarily focused on the listed LSE? Are your customers asking you why they cannot trade a Euronext stock on your exchange?

STUCHFIELD: They have asked us. But doing so is not a simple matter. Here is an example. There was a great deal of dissatisfaction in Holland. The Dutch trading community invited both Deutsche Börse and the LSE to come in and create separate

---

[4] Hooper's point is that MiFID, which came into effect Nov. 1, 2007 as the backbone of the E.U.'s single financial market, was intended to foster competition by eliminating barriers to this competition, such as the concentration of equity trade and price data in individual stocks on a single exchange. Under MiFID, that same data is supposed to be spread among multiple exchanges and other publication venues.

but parallel market to Euronext Amsterdam, the local Dutch market in cash equities. So, the LSE and Deutsche Borse each established their own markets so that there were, in effect, three parallel markets in Holland, if you include the Dutch market. We did the best that we could. I think that we did it rather successfully, mimicking the post-trade arrangements in clearing and settlement.

We significantly undercut the trading costs from an exchange perspective. But only between 1% and 10% of actual trading took place on our competitive platform. In the final analysis it was possible (I make this point generically rather than specifically) for the incumbent to defend its own market share by improving its own customer relations management, and by significantly reducing the cost of the exchange to the intermediary customer base.

To what extent can that customer request be relied upon in terms of actually following through and delivering the orders that would make the alternative market sustainable? I do not doubt that it is the same question that my colleagues on the panel face. There is no ITS in Europe which would make the link naturally sustainable. Ultimately, success is all about tipping liquidity from one market center to another. A state of bi-polar market centers, each of which has sustainable market share and liquidity, is probably not a model that would work.

PAGANO: There certainly is a lot of inertia to order flow. Once an exchange has a piece of the market it is hard to take it away even though you may have a better technological product.

STUCHFIELD: Yes, I agree. Ultimately the actual market structure features are very similar. It is possible to differentiate an open limit order book, as a number of us have done, by adding committed capital to it through market making programs and by hybridizing it. But ultimately it is a very similar model. Technology is quite similar across the exchanges, and the ability to differentiate is relatively limited.

PAGANO: Susanne, you had a comment?

KLOESS: Yes. Going back to the cash markets, Europe is very nationally driven. This is different from the U.S. The derivatives markets' products are more global. You can see differences in Europe where you have markets that are heavily trading in derivatives that are globally traded. We have been talking quite a bit about trading. Many people think that trading is a kind of "me too," you have to have it, you have to have your technology to support it. But look at it from a customer point of view, and consider the whole transaction in terms of one cost. Customers – investment banks, asset managers, traders – today spend a lot of money in the clearing and settlement arena. Where does the money go? It is the fees for trading compared to what they spend to actually get a trade settled and finally delivered.

There is a lot of discussion about a pan-European clearinghouse and what that would look like. Does that need one governmental structure, or could it be a kind of network where many places are linked? We are currently seeing in Europe that the move is more towards alliances and networks, rather than bringing it all under the umbrella of one governmental structure.

PAGANO: Yes Bob?

ROBERT SCHWARTZ [From the Floor]: Post-trade clearing and settlement is terribly important. I would like to ask the panel in general and you, Susanne, in particular, about the role that regulation plays in making it difficult. There simply is so much local regulation that is very different from locale to locale.

KLOESS: You are absolutely right, Bob. Regulation today, because it is still so national, is definitely a stumbling block. On the other hand, there is a strong push from the market participants to reduce cross-border settlement costs. This is where they spend a lot of money today. But my colleagues on the panel deal with this everyday, so I will pass the question on to them.

RECK: Just to give an example on the custody side, if you do corporate actions or stock splits or any type of custody services in equities or fixed-income products, you face different tax regimes in Europe. To serve the client adequately with payment and to execute his or her rights, you have to cope with all of these legislations in these different areas. That is outside the narrow regulation of securities markets, but it is also important for operations, for the efficiency of the costs that arise in that market.

PAGANO: Mark?

GUILLAUMIER: Commissioner McCreevy[5] has threatened exchanges with legislation unless they come to terms with clearing and settlement. It has become quite urgent.

STUCHFIELD: At this point, it is worth talking about the distinction between vertical and horizontal structures. The best way with an American audience to make this distinction is to look at the OCC, whose products are not owned by the exchanges that use it and therefore is able – in a completely independent way – to provide trading offsets and margin offsets between options products traded on, say, the ISE and on the CBOE. That is a horizontal structure.

    A good example of a vertical structure is the Chicago Mercantile Exchange. Merchandise that you trade on the Merc can only be cleared in the Merc clearinghouse. The Merc's value chain is fully integrated, and its economic model as a consequence is fully integrated. There are similar distinctions in Europe. Deutsche Börse has the vertical model, which it runs with some economic success, but not with a lot of customer adulation I think it would be fair to say.

RECK: Not a lot of what?

STUCHFIELD: Adulation, customer satisfaction (laughter)…

RECK: I wouldn't say so.

SCHWARTZ [From the floor]: Now the gloves come off.

STUCHFIELD: … at least in terms of the vertical nature of the model.

RECK: At least we have a strong growth in revenues.

STUCHFIELD: Indeed.

---

[5] Charles McCreevy is the European Union (EU) Commissioner for Internal Market and Services.

RECK: Our customers obviously like our services and ask us to extend them (laughter).

STUCHFIELD: The other end of the extreme would be the London Exchange, which has no ownership position in clearing or in settlement. Somewhere in between we have Euronext which is sort of half pregnant I think it would be fair to say (laughter). Euronext has an economic interest of 41% in the clearinghouse and a much much smaller percentage in Euroclear's CSD, or Central Securities Depository.

The cross-border complexity is greater in the settlement area. Yet both the International CSDs – and, increasingly, Euroclear as a CSD, which is equivalent to the Depository Trust Company in the U.S. – have managed to overcome all these national tax, regulatory and corporate actions issues. They have done it with some expensive technology. It is effective as far as the customers are concerned.

Clearing is the easier part from a cross-border regulatory and structural perspective. Rightly, the investment banking community wants to bring about a more enlightened structure than exists at the moment. However, a lot of the ownership issues around LCH Clearnet and Eurex Clearing stand in the way of that. It is a very complex issue. And it gets in the way of competition in the trading space.

BELLEGARDE: As you mentioned, Nic, a lot of harmonization on the clearing side has been done already between the four Euronext countries, France, Belgium, Holland and Portugal. Now this clearing is getting harmonized to the U.K., at least for the large-sized trades. If you look at the CSD side, you are right that Euroclear is also involved in harmonizing and streamlining the settlement part. Most of the time it is not a tax issue. We cannot sort tax issues out; they are too complex. But this is related to the investors and to the country each is in. This will not change. You can get to a level of harmonization and streamlining of settlement as long as you can refresh all of the rules and harmonize those rules. Most of those rules are laws. They are part of the exchange rules or regulatory rules. You have to do this work. It is very hard, very difficult work. But Clearnet has done it and Euroclear is finalizing it. They have a plan to get to one single settlement engine across the four countries by the end of 2007.[6] It is a long process. It is complex and costly. But it is a way to get to unified clearing and settlement in Europe.

PAGANO: Questions from the audience?

WILLIAM FREUND (Pace University) [From the Floor]: I have a question for the panel about European markets. To what extent are you feeling pressure, if any, for affiliations and mergers from your customers, from institutional investors, your stockholders, your management? What might be expected in the future?

BELLEGARDE: I will go back to the previous point. What do the shareholders and users require? The shareholders and the users, mainly large institutional investors and investment banks in London, are looking for a single European financial

---

[6] In March 2007, Euroclear said its single settlement engine (SSE) was successfully launched.

market. They want to overcome the complexities and the costs of trading cross-border. It is not that they cannot trade cross-border. They can and they do. They make a living out of it most of the time. But it still is very costly to develop that business. So their desire is not just to merge or to affiliate or to partner. Their only intention is to get one single European market. That is what they would like to have as users.

FREUND [From the Floor]: What about trans-Atlantic?

BELLEGARDE: As long as that would facilitate their business, they would be happy to do so. But they first want to look at Europe.

PAGANO: Another question?

MARC GRESACK (Matchpoint Trading) [From the Floor]: I have a question for Mark and Marcus. I am a poorly-informed American regarding MiFID. MiFID is fascinating. It addresses many issues that are similar to those being addressed in the U.S., order-handling rules being one of them. But I am curious. Are there also issues related to the Reg ATS rules, which were promulgated in the U.S. that allowed some intermediaries to compete with European exchanges?

HOOPER: I would start by not talking about MiFID. The regulation that you should think about more is the CP176 unbundling regulation.[7] That has the closest parallel to anything that I have seen. My understanding of the fairly recent comments from the SEC is that you will probably be moving down a similar path. While there are bound to be some complimentary areas with MiFID, I would look at unbundling as being the key area.

It is interesting how this has happened in the U.K. It looked like it would be a Big Bang event where suddenly the regulation came in on the first of January. But it looks like very little has changed in the short term. Of course, things can always happen, evolve, and change significantly over time. That is the regulation that I would take a closer focus on.

I do not know Reg ATS in sufficient detail to understand really close comparisons with some of the things that MiFID is trying to achieve under the harmonization. But, as I say, if you just think about the industry as a whole, the first thing that strikes me is the onset of technology and the integration of technology within the market structures. This is something that is just becoming obvious through MiFID. Regarding the best execution requirements, and the requirement to take on ancillary costs (I mean things like clearing and settlement costs that we have heard about), you will have to have some pretty hot technology on your desktop. It is not a simple matter to do all of the reconciliation that will be called for at the point of trading.

We are now talking about looking at more than just price at the point of trading. The debate has changed as the conversation continued on the various levels of MiFID that were being implemented. In the latest documentation, the European

---

[7] This regulation was introduced on Jan. 1, 2006 by the Financial Services Authority (FSA) in the U.K. as a result of the FSA's Consultation Paper 176 (CP176) on soft dollars. The new regulation governs the use of client commissions.

Commission has said very clearly that this is a trade-by-trade analysis. That is a most interesting example of where technology must have a major impact. I am sorry that I did not fully answer your question. But I would look at unbundling as the thing that has the most regulatory commonality.

ROBERT WOOD (University of Memphis) [From the Floor]: Are there cultural issues that mitigate against consolidation? For example, with the Daimler-Chrysler merger, within the first month trading was divided equally in New York and Germany. But four months later the order flow had essentially all moved to Germany. One of the key reasons was that most important management signals were coming out of Germany, and the German traders had a tremendous advantage over the U.S. traders in interpreting those signals. Would the Brits and the French be equally challenged in terms of interpreting signals coming out of Germany?

STUCHFIELD: There are cultural issues involved. I make this comment not about the London Stock Exchange, but about the City. The City is clearly the dominant financial center in Europe. It is the home of the largest share of asset management in Europe. However, London has always been incredibly open. Significant portions of the equity trading volumes that are driven from London are in German, or French equities, or those of the other Euronext countries, Scandinavia and the Iberian Peninsula. In some markets London-originated business accounts for over 40% of the volume.

London, like New York, has created a melting pot of different communities, traders and other securities professionals from all over Europe. London really does have a great ability to understand the signals that are coming out of other countries.

PAGANO: OK, very good. We are out of time. I want to thank the panel for their time and their very helpful insights (applause).

Chapter 3
Intermarket Competition: Trading Decisions

Bob Pisani, Douglas Atkin, Michael Cormack,[1] Alfred Eskandar,
David Harris,[2] and David Krell

ROBERT SCHWARTZ: It is a real pleasure to have Bob Pisani here to lead this panel for us. Bob, welcome to Baruch.

BOB PISANI: Thank you Bob. We have a very high-powered crowd here, and I do not mean just on the panel. I also mean in the audience. I see people who have been in this industry for a long time. I see people here who have shaped this industry. A lot of you people here are part of the future of this industry.

Let us start by talking about where this whole thing will end up. I have a simple theory. I call people all the time who are appalled that I am calling and asking such blunt questions, but as far as I can tell everybody is talking to everybody. That is the only way to understand what is going on. Some of our panelists can say a lot. Others may be under a few restrictions. If someone cannot answer something, I will ask someone else.

So, David Krell, when are you going to buy the New York Stock Exchange (laughter)? I mean when are you going to stop this namby-pamby stuff about, "I want to get into the equities business," and just let us know. It fits, doesn't it (laughter)?

DAVID KRELL: As you know, Bob, our policy is not to comment on M&A activities (laughter). But as you also know, I spent a lot of years at the New York Stock Exchange. That is all I will say. That is history.

PISANI: I was standing next to David the day the ISE went public. As a lot of you know, one of the great things about being at the New York Stock Exchange is some of the old traditions that exist down there. There is a tradition that the CEO always makes the first trade, usually a hundred shares – some nominal amount. So David came down for that. But you have to understand the irony – David left the NYSE a long time ago, and now here he is.

He is running his own business and it has become extremely important. Some would argue that derivatives are more important than the cash equities business. So,

---

[1] At the time of the conference, Mr. Cormack was Executive Vice President at the NYSE Group, Inc.

[2] At the time of the conference, Mr. Harris was Senior Vice President at the American Stock Exchange.

R.A. Schwartz et al. (eds.), *Competition in a Consolidating Environment*,
doi: 10.1007/978-0-387-75943-2_3, © Springer Science+Business Media, LLC 2008

I was standing there, and one of the privileges of being the floor reporter is that you get to stand next to all of these CEOs as they make their first trade. David was standing between me and John Thain. I turned to David and said, "Are you feeling nostalgic?" He looked at me and said, "It's good to be back" (laughter). He always was a very diplomatic gentleman.

Look, David, you have announced that you want to get into the equities business as well. I have lost count of how many competitors are potentially out there. There must be 15, 16, 17, maybe even 20, on an electronic exchange. What makes you think that you can make this work better than the other competitors out there?[3]

KRELL: We have consistently said that we are interested in broadening our horizons to other product areas. Equities are just one of those. We are interested in most others as well. The key for us is to identify a value proposition that is not being met. That is what we originally did with the ISE, and that is what we have identified here. It is a gap that we can walk into and seize the opportunity to broaden that market.

PISANI: Doug Atkin, what is driving all of this? Is it the globalization of the world equity markets? Is it regulation that is pushing it along? Is it new technologies? What is driving this intense consolidation? I have been on the floor for 10 years and, all of a sudden, you guys are the hottest thing on the planet. Your moment has come. Why now?

DOUGLAS ATKIN: It is just capitalism. Three years ago there were no publicly-traded exchanges in the United States. There were publicly traded ECNs, but not exchanges. The world is cottoning on to the fact that these are some of the most powerful, if not the most powerful, businesses in the world. They are natural monopolies. They are great businesses to run, and great businesses to own. Once an exchange gains dominant liquidity, it has tremendous amounts of pricing power. What is driving all of this consolidation is the fact that, once you have dominant liquidity, the good news is that no one can take it from you. The bad news is that you cannot take dominant liquidity away from anyone else. The only way for a cash equity market to trade other instruments effectively is through acquisitions. Or else to get into the derivatives business, or vice versa.

You will see huge consolidations over the next 2 years. The London Stock Exchange, again no surprise, will kick it off. Once that happens, it will be fun to get up in the morning and read *The Wall Street Journal*.

PISANI: But why (and anyone on the panel please jump in), why the London Stock Exchange? I know the arguments about Sarbanes-Oxley. I know the arguments that are put out there about it being more difficult to trade and to get listings in this kind of environment. I will throw this out to the panel in general. Maybe Alfred you can stick your two cents in here. Is Sarbanes-Oxley partly driving the interest in European exchanges at this point?

ALFRED ESKANDAR: I am not sure that I am the best guy on the panel to answer this one. We do not have any listings, and we are certainly not an exchange. There

---

[3] The ISE entered equity trading with the launch of the ISE Stock Exchange in September 2006.

have been articles left and right about a number of companies leaving U.S.-based exchanges because of the added expense of just complying. But I am not so sure if that is enough of a motive....

PISANI: Maybe Nasdaq wants to pursue it. They have got a position (laughter).

BRIAN HYNDMAN: Yes, I will take a crack at it. Nasdaq is always looking at acquisition opportunities that are strategic to our core business. Sarbanes-Oxley is one of the driving factors that led Nasdaq to look at the LSE. The number of IPOs in the U.S. has been down sharply over the past 4 years, and the foreign markets have been one of the beneficiaries. That is certainly one of the reasons that are driving exchanges to look at the LSE. Nasdaq is not the only one.

PISANI: What else will be driving change and competition here? I know that demutualization makes a big difference. All of sudden, when a company demutualizes and goes public, it seems to initiate some kind of increased transaction level. What else will be driving these motivations here?

HYNDMAN: There are two reasons why the exchanges and the markets are consolidating. One is what Doug Atkin mentioned, capitalism. When you have the exchange membership and the platform, you go out and acquire other exchanges and market share, and your business scales up nicely. The second is a regulatory reason. Look at 1997 when the order handling rules came out – suddenly all of the ECNs popped up. Now we have Reg NMS coming out, and that will lead to fragmentation by allowing all of these protected quotes to pop up around the country. Again, that leads to opportunities for acquisitions that will scale up your business.

PISANI: David and Mike, I want to bring you in on this. What is the end point here? Is it one exchange that trades multiple asset classes using single or several platforms? Where will we end up in the long term?

MICHAEL CORMACK: We are going in the direction of a one-technology platform and towards multi-products. You are starting to see that happen with competitors in the U.S. You see it a lot in Europe. In fact, many of the European exchanges are trading everything from a single stock all the way to the futures market. There are technology synergies and liquidity synergies. We can increase order interaction between equity options and plain vanilla equities. But equity exchanges are not getting into the futures business in the U.S.[4] While I agree with Doug that many

---

[4] The industry's demand for the trading of single stock futures in the U.S. waned after an initial flurry of interest earlier in this decade. This gained momentum with an agreement between the Securities and Exchange Commission and the Commodities Futures Trading Commission on initial and maintenance margin requirements. The expectation then was that several U.S. equity markets would enter the futures markets. Nasdaq planned this through Nasdaq Liffe (NQLX), a joint venture between itself and LIFFE, the derivatives exchange based in the U.K. Nasdaq later withdrew from this joint venture. Still, with margins on stock trading shrinking in this decade, U.S. exchanges were anxiously looking for new ways to satisfy shareholders. That is why trading in a variety of securities, both in the U.S. and overseas, was more acceptable to U.S. stock exchanges than in the past. The NYSE added the LIFFE futures market in London, when it completed its merger with Euronext in April 2007.

exchanges globally are monopolies, many are not. If you look in the U.S. at the cash equities business, and at the equities options business, there is definitely competition. There is competition between exchanges on both the options and the equities side, and there is a lot of competition from alternative trading systems like Liquidnet and Pipeline. The competition is truly robust.

Look at the futures market in the U.S. John Thain has commented publicly about the amiability of the Chicago Mercantile Exchange's business model.[5] There is a true monopoly in the products that they trade. I would argue that there are some really nice monopolies in the European cash equity markets. It is not simple. You have to look at each exchange in its own product niche, and figure out if it is a monopoly or not. Then, if it is not a monopoly, what is its order flow percentage, and where does it stand vis-à-vis the other exchanges and alterative trading systems that it is competing with. For the reason that Doug mentioned, all of these entities are looking more like businesses. It is capitalism. We are looking to leverage our platform, whether it is technology, or sales and distribution, or networks to produce more revenue generating transactions through those pipes.

DAVID HARRIS: The American Stock Exchange already is a multi-product exchange. For the last 2 years we have been developing a new trading platform that will enable us to put all of our products on the same platform. This will give us synergies across the different asset classes. I keep coming back to David's point. What is your value proposition? We understand from talking to customers that they already have the ability to electronically execute multiple asset classes from the front-end. So what is the value-added on the exchange side other than, perhaps, to give you, the customer, some price break? Maybe some order types – for example, a buy-write – that address certain trading problems.[6] It always comes back to two things: what does the customer want, and what is your value proposition?

PISANI: You are in an interesting position, David. The American Stock Exchange was a leader in the options business for many years. You were innovators in the exchange traded funds business, which is becoming more and more important. But you are losing market share in both of these important areas. How does that happen? How does it drift away from you? I know that you are talking about the platform, that you are hoping to bring that business back. But what will keep the people there?

HARRIS: Candidly, what happened to us is that we have good product development, but we took our eye off of the ball on the trading side. We developed and nurtured the ETF market, but when the product turned out to be better suited to electronic trading, we did not change our trading model and our technology quickly enough to maintain market share. We have learned from that lesson. The platform

---

[5] John Thain has publicly stated that the futures business in the U.S. is very attractive because it has higher margins than the cash business. He has noted the strong growth rates of various products traded by the Chicago Mercantile Exchange.

[6] This is a strategy that involves buying an underlying stock or index and writing – that is, selling – a call against it.

that we are developing now, and are well on our way to rolling out in time for Reg NMS, is fully electronic.[7] It will facilitate our current market structure. As products change throughout their life cycle, we will have the flexibility to trade one product in one market structure, and another product in a more appropriate market structure.

You mentioned that technology drives change. Technology is a key driver for many of the changes but the technology has become commoditized. Everyone has their own ECN now. How do you take advantage of some of the regulatory benefits that markets enjoy, but that broker-dealers do not? How do you merge your various value propositions to create a killer value proposition? Frankly, I do not know what the end state will look like, but I do know that it will include multi-asset classes. And it certainly will include very low-cost trading.

PISANI: David, did you want to add something?

KRELL: Yes. Everyone is focusing on multi-asset classes as if it is for the first time. I will call your attention to the fact that, when I was there, the New York Stock Exchange traded equities, options, bonds, and even futures. It was all under one roof. So it has been there before. At the Amex that certainly is still the case. They are trading multi-assets, but....

PISANI: But they let it drift away, David. I am sure that they regret it. They let it drift away. And here you are. Everybody is looking at you. If you are not looking at everybody else, everybody is looking at you. Why did that happen? Why did it drift away like that?

KRELL: I can tell you the story from the New York Stock Exchange's perspective. In 1997, when I sort of sold the options business (basically gave it away) to the CBOE, that business was not very attractive for any exchange. That sure has changed. In the last 5–6 years, options volume growth has been in excess of 24% per year. Now everyone is interested in it again.

PISANI: Why has the options business changed so much?

ATKIN: The options business is a few years behind the equity business in its evolution. The equity business is the first of the major market structure reforms, the first of the old auction markets to be restructured as electronic auction markets. Every traditional floor-based market that has implemented an ECN, or an electronic system, has kept its dominant liquidity pool. The exception to the rule of this natural monopoly is a market that never had a floor, or a traditional dealer market like Nasdaq. With its Instinet and Brut acquisitions, Nasdaq becomes a much more dominant player in the trading of its own stocks while, at the same time, the NYSE continues its leadership in listed stock trading. In the options market, maybe you should buy back the liquidity that the NYSE sold. But we think that the ISE is in a

---

[7] The American Stock Exchange announced on March 5, 2007 that its AEMI platform – an acronym for Auction and Electronic Market Integration – was fully rolled out and it complied with the trading phase of Reg. NMS, which commenced that same day. AEMI was launched on November 2006.

perfect position. It is analogous to the position that Nasdaq was in 4 years ago. There is lots of fragmentation and no dominant auction player. There are a lot of traditional markets. They will consolidate.

It is my belief that there will be one dominant liquidity pool for each equity option. It might be under one exchange. It might be two exchanges that split liquidity by instrument. But there is no tenable situation out there where exchanges at the end point will split liquidity say 50/50 or even 70/30.

PISANI: Does everyone agree with that? That there will be one dominant liquidity pool? That is a very provocative statement.

ESKANDAR: On the equity side, with the regulatory changes coming in under NMS, I do not agree with that. I think what happens will be driven by incentives customers are provided by exchanges and market centers in the coming Reg NMS environment. Reg NMS encourages best execution practices across all markets, so there is an onus on these exchanges and market centers to capture order flow consistent with customers' best price obligations. I would expect smaller markets to focus on reducing their trading costs, and to use those savings to induce order flow to come to their markets through the use of rebates. If you are incenting best price behavior, notwithstanding how large the other liquidity pool may be, order flow must come to you. And if you incent it aggressively enough, you can pretty much undercut anybody's liquidity pool.[8]

ATKIN: Exchanges are like eBay. If you have something to sell, you will go to eBay because you know that you will get a better price for your instrument. Even if a competing auction site entices you to auction off something for free, or pays you $5, the opportunity cost of being in a liquidity pool that has no liquidity is substantial. The losses that you will incur will far outweigh the benefits that you will get back on your commission. That is how I see it.

PISANI: Mike?

CORMACK: As much as I would like it to be true, I am not sure if a monopoly will be the end game. We are competing with each other for the options and equities businesses, and there are multiple ATSs out there competing for liquidity. We have not even talked about the internalization business that some people are worried will go from 30% to 50%. There are 30 broker-dealers out there trying to figure out profitable proprietary and internalization models. All of which will probably print off the exchange. There is a lot of competition out there for the order flow. But regulation can lead towards consolidation (via the trade-through rule, for instance).

Order delivery firms may not be comfortable sending their retail orders to an internalization engine if they are concerned about the trade-through rule. I do not

---

[8] BATS Trading, operator of an ECN founded in 2005, is an example. The growth in trading volume at this ECN is attributed in part to its aggressive rebate schedules. For example, at the start of 2007, in a special promotion, BATS paid more in trading rebates than it gathered in fees. BATS' average daily volume more than doubled in January. It matched just over 8% of all shares traded in Nasdaq stocks, up from 4% in the previous month.

know the answer to that question. We will see what happens when Reg NMS goes into effect. There is so much competition out there coming from so many different areas, that a natural monopoly in the equities or the options space is hard for me to buy into. I just do not see it happening.

PISANI: Mike, you brought up internalizing order flow. What are you doing to keep people down on the farm? David, you are starting a crossing system, didn't we talk about that?

KRELL: We are starting the ISE Stock Exchange. Can I make a comment about what Doug said about 70/30? In the option business, before competition ensued in 1999, it was even worse than that. It was 98 to 2. Even though there were the same contracts listed on multiple exchanges, 98% of the volume was typically at one exchange. It is only when real competition started between the markets that we more or less moved to the current state. We have about 34% market share, CBOE has about 35%, and everybody else has the rest. I do not see us going back to that predominant 90/10 or 70/30. As Mike said, there are lots of different trading strategies. There are lots of different reasons why the market will stay more or less fragmented.

What happened in the option market as a result of competition? Volume has soared. In 1999, the year before we came onto the scene, average daily volume for the entire industry was 1.7 million contracts a day. We (just ISE) traded 2.4 million contracts a day in the first quarter[9] of this year. That is the size that you see when competition comes on and is really real, rather than just displayed competition.

ROBERT WOOD (University of Memphis) [From the Floor]: I strongly agree with the comment that was made earlier that the real competition is competition for an order, not competition between exchanges to get listings. What David Krell has done in the options business is a classic example of the huge value of order-flow competition for the community. We have had a tremendous reduction in trading costs for options. You can go back to a time when, as Dave was saying, even though you had multiple listings on different exchanges, for whatever reason, one exchange always had the dominant position in an auction. The SEC put the spotlight on that, and we suddenly got competition. Then we suddenly had a reduction in trading costs.

My question is this: how is it that, in these securities markets which are at the core of our free market system, the New York Stock Exchange and Nasdaq have been able to buy their biggest competitors (laughter)?

PISANI: Anyone want to take that (laughter)? Mike, do you want to respond?

CORMACK: I cannot answer that question precisely. There has been a lot of discussion about decoupling where a product is listed and where it trades. We agree that we need to compete for the order. I came from the Arca side, and we competed

---

[9] Options trading on the ISE, which in April 2007 agreed to sell itself to Deutsche Börse AG for $2.8 billion, has grown since the conference. The ISE reported an average of 2.7 million contracts were traded in April 2007, a 14.7% percent increase over the same month a year ago. Overall, investors trading 54.6 million options at the ISE in April 2007, compared with 45.2 million contracts in April 2006, a 20.8% percent increase.

for every order that we ever got. It is important. At the same time, for the listings business, it is important to have a dominant market share in the products that are listed on your exchange. An example of that would be the acquisitions that Nasdaq made to get order flow in Nasdaq securities back under the Nasdaq umbrella. The Arca-NYSE merger was a little different because Arca's share in New York-listed names was not that significant.

PISANI: Doesn't it feel strange representing the NYSE (laughter)?

CORMACK: Not at all.

HYNDMAN: At Nasdaq we are a big fan of seeing orders compete. Nasdaq has the electronic model. It is fully transparent. Bids and offers and different market participants are competing out there based on price. That was the model which we created in 1971. We believe that that is the model going forward, especially for very liquid stocks. We see that New York's auction model is migrating to the dealer-based model. As Reg NMS fosters more competition, we see that our customers and other customers out there are going to a more transparent dealer market.

PISANI: Brian, you brought up Reg NMS. Obviously Reg NMS is accelerating the move to electronic trading. Once the NYSE goes through with its hybrid system, and goes to electronic trading, will it be easier to trade NYSE stocks? I presume it will be.

HYNDMAN: Certainly it will. We see that it is easier today. Reg NMS was announced a little over a year ago. Our customers started connecting to our electronic pools of liquidity. They were demanding the immediacy and the transparency of the electronic market. You can see that New York's market share dropped from 80% down to 68% if you are not counting Arca's order flow.[10] Our touch business[11] went from somewhere around 3% up to about 20%. So it seems like customers are demanding the immediacy and the efficiency of the electronic model.

ATKIN: We do a lot of work on parsing out volume between exchanges. We would argue that the only volume which really adds to enterprise value for investors is that which is matched on an order book, or else is specialist volume during market hours when exchanges compete. Nasdaq is talking, as they should, about 20% market share. If you really parse the volumes out and look at New York market share versus Nasdaq share in NYSE listed stocks, Nasdaq has only 8% of NYSE stocks.

---

[10] As of October 2007, the New York Stock Exchange matched some 40% percent of the volume of all NYSE-listed trades, according to industry analyst Richard Repetto and published statistics.

[11] Hyndman is referring to Nasdaq's "'touched'" trade executions. Nasdaq says these "touched' trades represents total share volume of Nasdaq or NYSE-listed securities executed on the Nasdaq Market Center and the INET book – plus volume of shares routed to other market centers for execution – as a percentage of consolidated Nasdaq or NYSE market volume. Nasdaq reported that touched market share in NYSE-listed securities rose to 33.3% percent in December 2006, from 31.5% percent in November and 16.1% percent December 2005.

HYNDMAN: The trend in Nasdaq's trading of NYSE-listed stocks is the same though. Our market share is growing.[12] We calculate our numbers in three ways: We have our venue; we our touched (New York calls it handled); and then we have our reported numbers. If you take a look, what we were doing on our venue 2 years ago was less than 2%. Now it is up to 8%. So the trend is pretty much the same.

ATKIN: But that gain is through acquisitions. What we are seeing in our data is that you are making moderate gains. Please do not get me wrong, but the gains are very moderate.

HYNDMAN: It cannot be through acquisition if the NYSE went from 80% down to 68%.

ATKIN: It did because a lot of that is trading on Arca.

HYNDMAN: Maybe if it went from 80% down to 73%.

ATKIN: Not in matched order volume. That is my only point. That is the only volume that counts.

PISANI: Now we are really getting down to the nitty-gritty here (laughter). It is all about order flow. If you have got it, you have got respect. If you do not have it, they will fight you for it (laughter).

NIC STUCHFIELD (London Stock Exchange) [From the Floor]: The essence of Doug's point is that you cannot successfully compete on price alone. I would agree with that.

PISANI: You have had some experience with that, Nic.

STUCHFIELD [From the Floor]: Well, indeed, I have. I have had experience both at Tradepoint and in Holland with the LSE. Where competition has been successful, it was because there have been significant structural changes. One obviously thinks about onscreen market making at the ISE versus at the CBOE. One thinks of the Bund contract going from LIFFE to the DTB (which is now Eurex). Aside from the ISE with its Mid-Point Match (which is clearly a structural innovation), what will the other three exchanges on the panel do to increase the competitive structural differentiation between one another?

PISANI: Mike, David, Brian?

HARRIS: That is a very complex question for us. Look at the products that we currently trade. We own a very large percentage market share of the current Amex-listed products. And to David's point before, exchanges will be constantly looking at how to expand their product base. We have looked at how we will get more fully into the Nasdaq and New York space. As I said before, in a post-Reg NMS world, if you can incent best price behavior, then order flow will have to come to you.

---

[12] Nasdaq says its overall market share in the volume of NYSE stocks traded – as distinct from its touched trades market share – was 15.5% percent, as of April, 2007, compared with a year ago share volume of 8% percent. Nasdaq's touched market share measures its "matched" shares and the shares Nasdaq routes to other venues. This touched market share is also one level of trading activity that generates transaction revenue for Nasdaq.

While we can talk about how good this is for public customers, exchanges very much will become utilities for their users.

As Mike said, there is a lot of competition out there. Everyone cringes when you are a publicly-traded company. However, to get market share, you have to compete on cost. It is a scary world when your differentiating factor is price. We will get into the space by incenting people with the highest rebates possible. If you do it the right way, you can make money on your order flow when you provide liquidity. It will hurt other markets in terms of their market shares.

HYNDMAN: It comes down to three critical components: speed, price and liquidity. Speed is ultra important when you have different models trading against one another. Look at some of our speed times. You can get an order done in less than 10 milliseconds nowadays. I will repeat that: not 30 s, not 500 ms, but in less than 10 ms. Price, as David mentioned, is a critical factor. It is something that we all compete on every day, whether it is the rebate that we give, or a take-out charge.[13] And ultimately, it comes down to liquidity. Depending on your speed and price, can you get that order executed on that exchange? If you do not have those three components – speed, price and liquidity – you are not even in the game.

ESKANDAR: I agree with you, Nic. You certainly cannot just compete on price alone. In fact, because there is so much innovation coming to market now, to compete you really have to change the rules of the game. You almost have to change the structure in which you offer value back to the client. I find it interesting that I am sitting on this panel with the national exchanges. It took me a while to understand why. Part of it is because the majority of the stuff that we trade we tend to trade more than the actual national exchanges in those names. As a result, we are actually becoming our own significant market center by default.

Value has to start from understanding the customer base. There is not just one type of customer out there. There is not just one type of trader. You certainly do not need one type of offering. The institutional base and the retail base have been very different. There are a lot of different types of institutions that trade rapidly and in smaller increments, trying to mimic retail- type accounts. But, at the end of the day, there is a move to offer value for the wholesale trader, for the institutions, and for the block orders. You see a lot of systems coming out offering block capabilities. Why? Because there has been a big void. Systems like the one we run have proven that this can be a viable business, that this can grow substantially and, more importantly, that this can also be global.

The theme today, as Bob has put it together, is global competition, global capabilities. We trade in 13 different markets. It is the same model. You start with customer needs. Then you try to differentiate yourself by changing the rules of the game. In that way, hopefully, you can build a pretty strong offering.

PISANI: Mike?

---

[13] The "take-out" charge is the term used to describe the Nasdaq fee traders pay for executing orders – that is, electronically taking-out shares – on Nasdaq itself. It is the opposite term for "rebates," which Nasdaq pays traders for adding shares – that is, liquidity – to its system.

CORMACK: I do not know what the term "commodity business" means any more. If you look at our space, I do not think that you have ever seen a pure commodity business model. Look at Island, which started out 6 or 7 years ago with what, at the time, was probably the lowest-priced platform. Nevertheless, Island differentiated itself with its technology implementation. The Island platform was awesome. It was unlike anything the equity markets had ever seen before. Yes, it was cheap, but it was also really good. Now I get a little worried. I heard that Josh Levine[14] is trying to build a matching engine for 150 grand, but I also hear that he is now working on solar power (laughter)...

Setting that option aside, we can differentiate ourselves in lots of different ways. Is it difficult to explain to my grandfather what the difference is between Arca's trading platform and Nasdaq? Yes, it absolutely is. But it is not hard to explain to someone who is sitting on a trading desk. Look at what has happened overseas. Look at what has happened in the futures market. Every exchange has enabled itself to develop new products and to differentiate itself in any number of ways. Just like every broker-dealer in this room tries to differentiate itself for its institutional clients, or for its retail clients.

I am often asked about pricing and "Johnny-come-lately" ECNs. Let me say this much: it is important to remember that even though customers could potentially pay a marginally lower rate for their execution business at one of these new destinations, I would be hesitant to move all my order flow from an exchange platform to one of these ECNs, if I was in the customers' shoes. After all, several of the large exchanges have invested millions of dollars in capacity, redundancy and disaster recovery. Many of our customers operate multi-hundred million dollar a year businesses connected with our systems. I do not think they are real eager to jump to the latest ECN of the month. These customers are business people and they understand our value as long as we provide rational pricing for them. Of course, there are big businesses that are running on all of these ECN platforms and destinations that are very important to the broker-dealer community, and to the institutional community. They will continue to fight with one another and obviously there will be new entrants. We have seen six or seven new entrants in just the last 18 months.

PISANI: Some more questions?

UNIDENTIFIED SPEAKER [From the Floor]: You were all just talking about electronic trading as if it is completely appropriate for every single stock that we trade. I think we all know that it is probably appropriate for roughly the top 200 stocks in each of our marketplaces (or perhaps the top 100 stocks). How do you all plan to compete against something like what I do on the exchange floor with the less liquid stocks? When I speak to my customers they tell me that it is not really that great trading the smaller stocks on an electronic market.

ESKANDAR: I can take a shot at this one. Eighty percent of what we do is small and mid-cap...

---

[14] Josh Levine, co-founder of Island ECN, is regarded as a talented computer programmer.

UNIDENTIFIED SPEAKER [From the Floor]: I will just say that you may be somewhat of an exception (laughter).

ESKANDAR: Okay, I am sorry. Next (laughter).

UNIDENTIFIED SPEAKER [From the Floor]: The reason I say that is because, if I am correct, you may be an exception because you are primarily a block trading facility, correct?

HYNDMAN: I will take a shot at that. We think that the electronic model is best for the Nasdaq, top 200, 500, whatever the number is. But we are also coming out with our block crossing network, which we call the Intra-Day Cross. With it, we will match off large institutional orders that come in via their brokers at the mid-point. We understand that there is a need to have some kind of block crossing mechanism for some of these less liquid stocks. Accordingly, we plan on launching the Intra-Day Cross in early'07.[15]

UNIDENTIFIED SPEAKER: But what about the people who do not trade blocks?

HYNDMAN: It doesn't necessarily have to be a block. There could be a minimum requirement, but the minimum does not have to be 10,000 shares.

UNIDENTIFIED SPEAKER [From the Floor]: You will be printing smaller lots, just matching them.

HYNDMAN: We could do that, yes.

PISANI: There are plenty of people who cross by consolidating many orders at once. Isn't that possible as well?

HYNDMAN: Yes.

ESKANDAR: Floor brokers are brokers, they are not exchanges. What has happened in other markets? Here is an anecdote from London. When London went from its auction market to its SETS system in 1997 (SETS is an electronic trading system), a lot of brokerage firms did not think that it would happen, particularly in small and mid-cap stocks. They did not even get office space above the floor. But in two weeks it was over. Every stock had gone electronic. That does not mean, however, that there is still no room for brokers in the upstairs market.

Our view is that Pipeline is competing in the brokerage space, in the block trading space, above the floor. But Pipeline does not compete with the national markets. It will not unless it gets up to 80% market share. If so, then it is its own market. But there is no public pricing mechanism in Pipeline.

We are seeing LaBranche make a similar move, as did Knight Trading. I think that floor brokers will have to differentiate themselves away from the floor.

UNIDENTIFIED SPEAKER: No, I don't think so (laughter).

---

[15] On June 5, 2007, NASDAQ announced the launch of its Intraday Cross (as well as Post-Close Cross.) The Intraday Cross was designed for institutional-sized orders seeking liquidity and anonymity.

PISANI: That was a cynical remark. Mike, maybe you could bring us up to date on hybrid. I do not know how much you are paying attention to it, or if it is in your bailiwick or not. We are supposed to be rolling things out here, and we are having a gradual rollout already on the floor. The e-broker is already rolled out. What does the timetable look like? Also tell us, is it really obvious that highly liquid stocks are not only going to trade away from the floor, but that they will even trade away from the NYSE?

CORMACK: First of all, I am definitely involved in the hybrid. It is a huge resource demand within the organization, and everyone is watching it. Second, last I checked, the next big launch will be in the August-September time frame. It would probably be good to ask Cathy Kinney about this later today. That will be for firms off the floor and institutional clients using direct market access (DMA) products.

Some pretty substantive changes will come out in that timeline. Beyond that, the system is designed to take on the attributes of the floor broker and the specialists, and to put those together with the 75% market share that we have in those names. Incidentally, our market share is higher in the small and mid-cap zone, which tells you that perhaps there is some value-added by the floor interaction in these lower liquidity areas. We will continue to work on that platform.

In keeping with what has been designed and discussed to date, there will be multiple phases, just as there were to the Archipelago trading platform. We change these things. They evolve based upon what our clients want us to do. We will continue to add new functionality. We really want to retain it. As I said earlier, it is very important that we retain our market share. We believe that the floor adds value in the liquidity process and in the price discovery process, and we will continue to fight it out in that realm.

PISANI: Mike, when is the end product, the final rollout, going to be seen? When will we see the specialists employing their algorithms, along with full interaction between the floor and the ECNs?

CORMACK: The most substantive changes, outside of the floor community, will be in the August-September period. When will we have specialists' algorithms and other trading functionality available, along with more of an auto-ex? When will we see the last rollout? There will be a rollout every six months, or every quarter forever, whether we are adding new block trading functionality, or a new tweak for the floor broker community, or any number of things. We have releases going well into next year on both the hybrid system, the Arca listed, the OTC equity platforms, and the options platforms. These things are not static. We are always watching what David or Brian is doing. Sometimes we are reacting, and sometimes we are defining new territories.

PISANI: We only have a few minutes left, so let's get down to some brass tacks. Doug Atkin, you are paid to think big picture. What is the next big deal going to be?

ATKIN: The London Stock Exchange. That is the premier brand in Europe. It is the only brand. You have to define the strength of an exchange's brand by what it can command in listing fees. The only exchange in Europe that can command any kind of listing fees is the London Stock Exchange.

PISANI: Why not the Deutsche Börse? It has an integrated platform. It has a great clearing business. That to me seems like an even more interesting proposition. But everyone is talking about London at this point. Why is that?

ATKIN: There is clearly a different battle between listings and trading. If you can increase your listings revenues by 25% or 30% a year, that goes straight to the bottom line, and these exchanges are publicly-traded entities. Again, they are natural monopolies. So the exchange that does not get the LSE, be it Nasdaq or the NYSE, basically has to write off the UK market. No one has been able to wrestle dominant liquidity away from UK trading. Tradepoint tried it. No one has been able to wrestle away listings.

Just one final point. Amy was far and away the best financial analyst on the Street when she was at CSFB. But I will disagree with you about something, Amy. I said that Instinet at 30% market share was an untenable situation. The tenable end point is investors owning an entity that has 100% market share. Unless you can get up to 60% and hit the tipping point, it is tough.

PISANI: So who will win the battle for the LSE?

ATKIN: I think New York.[16]

PISANI: Why?

ATKIN: Maybe Nic can answer it better than I can (laughter).

PISANI: Well, if somebody wants to give me a reason, go ahead.

ATKIN: I was fortunate enough to spend 6 years in Europe and, by and large, New York has a better brand. It can command higher listing fees. The city of London in general, and I believe the LSE in particular (all other things being equal), would rather do a deal with the Americans than with the continental Europeans. Within the U.S. equity exchanges, I believe that the LSE would rather do a deal with New York than with Nasdaq.

PISANI: If anyone else wants to get in on this, please do. After that, what happens (laughter)?

ATKIN: I am the only one without an ax to grind these days. It is really interesting to hear Mike talk about the hybrid (laughter).

PISANI: I told you, you don't appreciate the irony.

ATKIN: I think it will touch off a wave of consolidation. After New York or Nasdaq buys London, the loser will go and buy one of the European exchanges, Deutsche Börse or Euronext. Or Deutsche Börse and Euronext will merge.

PISANI: What about the derivatives exchanges in the U.S., and the regional exchanges?

ATKIN: I will let someone else answer that.

---

[16] On April 4, 2007, NYSE Euronext was launched. It is the holding company created by the combination of NYSE Group, Inc. and Paris-based Euronext NV. Nasdaq's $5.3 billion hostile bid for the London Stock Exchange, was rejected earlier in 2007.

PISANI: Well, panelists, you are all sitting there staring at me. Go ahead guys, where do you think this will end up? (Silence). Okay, that was great (laughter). Alfred?

ESKANDAR: I think that major acquisitions are on the horizon. There will be acquisitions within asset classes and across asset classes.

PISANI: Why isn't the CME doing more? They have this big pile of stock that they are sitting on. Why aren't they doing more? I had this guy on the other day from the CME, and he just looked like he wished he was not there when I asked him for his thoughts about the exchange (laughter). Why isn't more happening with the Chicago Mercantile Exchange? It seems to me that they are in a particularly strong position. They are sitting out there with their natural monopoly (or whatever they have) and they say nothing.

ESKANDAR: All right, I will talk about it. Liquidity is the CME's natural monopoly, but the icing on their cake is owning the vertical integration of the clearing system. There is a reason why the CME has not done any acquisitions to date. Because of their vertical integration, they have been able to take products that are traded in the dealer market OTC. Because of the domination of their clearing vehicle, they have been able to bring those products on the exchange. That is a serious growth strategy for a futures exchange that has its own clearing system. The equities markets (particularly the U.S. and U.K. markets) do not own their own clearing systems. As I said, the only way to grow is through pricing increases. I think that the CME will put in serious price increases. They will also grow through acquisitions.

PISANI: Finally, what about the regional exchanges? What happens to Philly? What happens to Boston?

HARRIS: I will answer that. The smaller exchanges compete. The changes that are occurring on the regulatory and technology side allow us to do that. When I look at the consolidations, I can understand why publicly-traded companies need consolidation to grow. But to get back to Amy's point, what is the value proposition? How do consolidations actually help your customers? It does not do your business any good if you lose sight of who you are serving.

KRELL: I want to clarify something that Doug talked about earlier. Nic also mentioned it in a previous panel. I am referring to horizontal and vertical integration in the structure of exchanges today. I do not believe that these two separate models properly explain what drives the business of these exchanges today. An example of vertical integration is Deutsche Börse, which trades securities and commodities and, at the same time, clears and settles securities under the same umbrella, or in the same silo. On the other hand, the options exchanges in the U.S. have a horizontal model – clearing is centralized at the Options Clearing Corp. (OCC). The substance of the business models (what drives the economics of these exchanges) is actually whether or not the products traded are fungible. The five option exchanges in the U.S. own the OCC. But in 1975 the SEC mandated that every option created in the U.S. be a product that is fungible. That means you can buy an options today at the ISE and sell the exact same option on one of the other five exchanges. Clearly, every stock is also fungible. That is what drives the economics of the stock trading business. It is not that the Chicago Mercantile Exchange owns its own clearing operation. I do not think that has anything to do with the underlying strength of its economic model. It is the fact that there is no competition, because the CME trades a non-fungible asset.

ATKIN: Why do you think it is non-fungible?

KRELL: It is non-fungible because they like it that way.

ATKIN: Right, but someone else would like to get in and trade…

KRELL: It is a contract. Even if you have the same terms in your contract, one organization can simply choose not to abide by those terms because it is a non-fungible asset. In the futures markets, you could have two virtually identical futures, but because they are not issued by the same clearing corporation, they are not fungible. So you do not have competition in the futures industry. I was trying to get into the futures business. It is far more difficult on the futures side to leverage liquidity because of this non-fungibility.

PISANI: We have to leave it there. One thing I can assure you is that we will be here 1 year from now, and this whole game will be completely different. I have been a business reporter for 16 years now, and I do not remember when I have seen this business being more dynamic and more exciting. You guys are right here in the heart of one of the most important areas of the business world today. Thank you all for coming (applause).

Chapter 4
Intermarket Competition: Listing Decisions

Jamie Selway, Noreen Culhane, John Labuszewski, John McGonegal,[1]
and William O'Brien

JAMIE SELWAY: As our exchanges have graduated from member-driven coopera-
tives, and have invested in for-profit companies, attention has turned to questions
such as; what do our exchanges do, what kinds of businesses are they in, and what
are their prospects?

Historically, our exchanges have performed three functions: They have listed
securities, traded these securities, and sold the associated market data. Our panel
will explore the listings business. As we heard from the last panel, listings, which
are one of the more attractive sides of exchanges, account for about a third of their
revenues. We will hear from the NYSE and NASDAQ about their value propositions for companies they list. Finally, creating new equities is a dimension of the
listings business, so we will hear from the AMEX about its business in Exchange
Traded Funds, options and other instruments. We will also hear about other instruments from the Chicago Mercantile Exchange.

Yes, we have someone here from the CME. We can all pile on him in a Q&A.
They have a very different approach to creating new products. It is also a different
regulatory environment.[2] With that said, I would like each panelist to briefly
explain their listings business and value propositions. Then we will have the Q&A
with a couple of questions from me and then from the audience.

We should note that the NYSE is in the midst of a quiet period with its secondary
offering.[3] So Noreen will let us know when we stray into areas that are off limits
for her at this time as she answers our questions. Please welcome Noreen Culhane
of the NYSE Group.

NOREEN CULHANE: The New York Stock Exchange has been in the listings
business for many, many years. The exchange, as most of you know, is almost as

---

[1] At the time of the conference, Mr. McGonegal was Senior Vice President at the American Stock
Exchange.

[2] The Chicago Mercantile Exchange is a self-regulatory organization overseen by the Commodity
Futures Trading Commission. The Securities and Exchange Commission has oversight for U.S.
stock exchanges.

[3] The NYSE began trading under ticker symbol, NYX, in March 8, 2006. That was soon followed
by a secondary offering of stock, which facilitated holders of exchange seats who had to honor
certain lock-up provisions.

R.A. Schwartz et al. (eds.), *Competition in a Consolidating Environment*,
doi: 10.1007/978-0-387-75943-2_4, © Springer Science+Business Media, LLC 2008

old as the country itself, having been founded in 1792. We are very proud today, as a newly-public company, to continue our focus on our listings business. We trade 2,700 of what we consider the world's best companies. They have an aggregate market valuation of $22 trillion, so we are the largest market in the world, by a significant factor. On an average day we trade 1.7 billion shares of those listings.

Our listings business changed with the acquisition of Archipelago. We now have a second listing platform that is a key component of the NYSE. If we measure our success in new listings, the IPO market is a good place to start. In the IPO market today, and over the last 5 years, we have been able to target about 30% of the companies that enter the public market. That is the percentage that meets our standards. Of those companies, we succeed in attracting 90% (or in excess of 90%) of the qualified proceeds that are raised within that group. We have a very strong business here even though we are only approaching a third of the market.

With out new listing standards, we will basically be able to approach two-thirds of the market. That is because we are creating, or have created, listings standards for the Archipelago platform that will allow us to look at another 30% of the new IPO market. What is the value proposition across the two platforms? We think there are three major components. One, clearly, is the quality of the market provided. In terms of quality, we look at liquidity, intra-day volatility, and transaction costs – generally speaking, the cost of capital. We measure that relentlessly and rigorously, as you might imagine. It is, sort of, the crown jewel. We believe that we provide the best market in the world in terms of the deepest liquidity, dampened volatility, and low transaction costs. We are proud of that. Importantly, third parties such as Plexus, Elkins/McSherry, Abel/Noser and the Securities and Exchange Commission itself, as well as several academic studies, would support our conclusions.

We believe that the specialist plays a key role, not just in providing provisional liquidity, but also in the second major component of the value proposition – access to information. Through the exchange and the tools we provide, as well as what the specialist does and in the Arca platform, we are creating a lead market maker (LMM), an electronic version, if you will, of a specialist. This lead market maker will designate an individual to make a market in each security traded on the Arca platform and, at the same time, to also provide insight by phone and other means to the listed company into trading activity in the company's stock.

Lastly, I want to mention services. Our listed companies look to the exchange not only to provide an excellent trading venue and an excellent market (and market quality), but also to provide services as they reach out to the investing public, both institutional and retail. There are several conferences that we sponsor, or support, both on the institutional and the retail side, domestically and internationally. We run virtual investor forums. We created password-protected Websites to provide information to our companies, not just about trading, but also on corporate governance. The list goes on and on. I would say that the three major components of the value proposition are high quality markets, access to information, and robust portfolio services.

SELWAY: Bill O'Brien, could you compare and contrast NASDAQ's offering to that?

WILLIAM O'BRIEN: I will start by acknowledging that, in the listings competition business, the customer base is playing a bit of catch up. Customers are just starting to become sensitized to the fact that they have a choice. Frankly, they have an obligation to periodically evaluate their choice of listings markets. The fact that you have been listed on a particular venue for 10, 25, or 100 years is in many ways irrelevant to where you should be listed in the future. That is not the impression that most listed company executives had 5 or 10 years ago. But today, many of these executives are aware of it. That probably comes from how exchanges, and the perceptions of exchanges, have evolved. People are no longer viewing us as just another regulator. They are looking to their listings market to be a true vendor partner. That plays to any exchange with a strong value proposition that meets high thresholds of brand legitimacy and regulatory integrity like the NYSE and NASDAQ. Once you achieve that, then I agree with Noreen completely. It comes down to a value proposition based on these tenets: performance, price, service and visibility.

From a performance perspective, we are talking about the quality of our market as well. The introduction of exchange execution quality data – under Reg NMS Rule 605 – has, for the first time, allowed listed companies to do an objective apples-to-apples comparison of the quality of an exchange's market structure. The trading community has been using these stats for some time. The issuer community is starting to become more focused as well as educated about the stats, and are aware of their responsibility to evaluate the impact on their investors. When you use these stats for a true comparison of the markets free from any institutional bias, NASDAQ's market structure – with complete end-to-end automation, robust competition, and total transparency – is winning consistently on the spread, on speed, and on the number of trades executed at, or better than the quoted spread.

NASDAQ competes fairly aggressively on price. Pricing, however, should not be about how many dollars you can suck out of your customers. At NASDAQ, we try to deliver real value. NASDAQ has materially lower listing fees on an initial, and an ongoing basis. Its event-driven fees are also lower, like the listing of additional shares. Then there is the service dynamic. From our perspective, we have three prongs of service: A dedicated relationship manager; NASDAQ Online and our market intelligence desk. The relationship manager is your point of contact if you are a listed company, CEO, CFO, or IR director. NASDAQ Online is our industry leading electronic platform for our listed companies that want to see the current and historical trading information in their stock, and other information.

The market intelligence desk aims to provide our listed companies with the next level of trading color, such as information on why their stocks are trading as they are. This requires combining all the proprietary information that we have as an exchange operator, along with the best available information from other sources. This desk not only looks at the trading of a listed company's stock, regardless of whether it is the 80% of the time that the trade happens on NASDAQ. It also looks at the stock of a company's peers, regardless of where those peers are listed.

Combine all of this with the great visibility for companies listed on NASDAQ, such as MarketSite – our seven floor tower at Times Square seen by over 1.5 million visitors per day, NASDAQ.com with two million unique visitors per day – and you can see why we are offering a package that companies are finding more and more compelling. One of the most telling stats, from my perspective, is that, for the first time in history, there were more NYSE companies beginning a relationship with NASDAQ than the other way around, either through our dual listing program or switching to NASDAQ outright. This is revolutionary when you consider the historical notion of where NASDAQ and the NYSE stood within the landscape of U.S. exchanges. And larger companies are finding NASDAQ superior as well. If you look at the size of switchers from a market capitalization perspective, that ratio is ten to one in favor of NASDAQ. That is only one data point, but it is more reflective of the fact that issuers realize that they have a choice, and are taking their obligation to evaluate their choice more seriously than ever before.

SELWAY: John McGonegal, in addition to companies, AMEX is truly a multi-product exchange. You guys created the Exchange Traded Funds (ETFs), and you list options. Can you talk a bit about your business?

JOHN MCGONEGAL: On the equities side, we are really focused on small mid- and even micro-cap companies. Just to give you an example, the largest company that we listed last year had just about a billion dollars in market cap. The biggest company that we have listed so far this year is about $75 million. We really only became aggressive in terms of promoting ourselves on the equity front about 3 years ago.

To put some numbers in perspective: Last year we listed some one hundred companies, and we should exceed that number this year. In the past we really only focused on domestic companies. We then started to branch out and looked to our partners up north in Canada where we have been very successful. We recently hired a director for business development in both Israel and Europe. In fact, I was in Israel last week for the exchange. Over the next several months we will have more meetings in London and one in Calgary.

We position ourselves as a small marketplace with high levels of service, whether it is a full suite Investor Relations package paid for at our expense, online targeting tools, or dedicated relationship managers. Then again, with regard to some of the statistics and reports that Noreen was pointing to, we can show quantitatively that the specialists can add value in these small and mid-cap companies.

On the ETF side, we look to be partners with our issuers, whether it is with index creation, product creation, or helping them go through the regulatory hurdles and get products up and trading. We have a separate marketing staff devoted to ETFs, be it going out and talking to traders, analysts, potential issuers, and even so far down the food chain as going out to branch offices and talking about the benefits of ETFs.

If you look at how we position ourselves, it is very simple. We are a small, niche player. There is a place for us, whether it is high levels of service, offerings, and a very flat, lean organization. We think that we can compete with a few strong products.

SELWAY: John Labuszewski of the CME. Can you talk a bit about CME's highly successful new product efforts?

JOHN LABUSZEWSKI: It was not too long ago that futures and financial futures were considered the poor provincial cousins of the financial services industry. It is a happy day when we are invited to participate in a prestigious event like this. Let me suggest then, at the risk of reciting the company line, that the CME prides itself and believes that its success in recent years is directly attributable to the fact that it has always maintained what we regard as the three pillars of the CME: financial integrity, liquidity, and innovation. It is that last pillar that I would like to discuss today.

The CME has a long history of innovation. The CME invented financial futures with the introduction of currency futures in 1972. We were also pioneers in another respect: We introduced the concept of cash settlement in 1981 when Eurodollar futures were launched. I believe we were the first futures exchange to make widespread use of electronic trading technologies when we introduced Globex back in 1992.[4] The Globex platform has grown to become the most widely distributed, and we believe the most effective, electronic trading platform worldwide in derivatives trading.

When I first saw the topic of today's discussion – listings – I had to step back a bit and say, wait a second, we do not list new products at CME, rather we create new products– futures contracts and options contracts. Each futures contract that we develop is unique. Many of the features that have been pioneered at the CME actually have been adopted and utilized worldwide in many other markets. When we talk about listings, we believe we are talking about a form of creativity. Frankly, new product development is the life-blood of our exchange. And we have a long record of success on this score.

SELWAY: I will start with a few questions, and then we will jump to the audience. This is for NASDAQ and New York in particular: How will the exchange business change over the next couple of years? You know, we have read some interesting news stories lately on New York merging with Archipelago. The NYSE, consequently got, sort of an NYSE Junior Varsity, or an NYSE lite. NASDAQ has made some interesting headway, selling D&O insurance; and building an independent network of research providers.[5] What do you see on the new product end for the issuer services business?

---

[4] Globex, launched in 1992, is regarded as the first global electronic futures trading platform. It now trades products like stock index and currency futures.

[5] On Sept. 7, 2005, NASDAQ agreed to acquire Carpenter Moore Insurance Services, when it entered a definitive agreement with the privately held San Francisco-based insurance brokerage specializing in management liability, such as Directors and Officers ("D&O") insurance. NASDAQ's customer base was issuers. NASDAQ also launched the Independent Research Network (IRN) around this same period with Reuters. IRN provided research coverage for small and mid-cap companies, filling a gap created when large brokers ended coverage in the wake of regulatory reforms in 2002. However, in late 2007, NASDAQ and Reuters decided to shut down the venture. A spokesperson for NASDAQ described the adoption rate as "slower than anticipated."

O'BRIEN: When you speak about products and services, first look at it from the purely commercial perspective of NASDAQ, the NYSE, or any other publicly-traded company. Some of the earlier panels were asked where revenue growth will come from. This is an opportunity for that to happen. NASDAQ has relationships with CEOs and CFOs. This amounts to a rolodex of names that almost any business would kill for. That said, Noreen's point a little earlier is that the ability to deliver a product to our listed companies only makes sense if we can tie it back to our core value proposition. We have acknowledged that we have a level of scale and competency that can make the task of being a listed company easier and less expensive over time, as that process gets harder every day for some competitors and other companies. We are achieving scale and competency through acquisition (most recently with our acquisition of Shareholder.com[6] and Carpenter Moore), and through partnerships with the likes of Reuters for the provision of independent research. I have sat at many meetings of soon to be public companies with CFOs who had bags under their eyes bigger than mine, and they had a long list of things to accomplish just to get to their IPO dates. Then the real work begins of maintaining public company status. As an integrated solutions provider, we help you check the boxes, whether it is with Shareholder.com – an award-winning customizable investor relations Website – and other communication tools; or through the NASDAQ insurance agency – augmented by Carpenter Moore – offering D&O, E&O and other insurance coverage. From a visibility perspective there is IRN, NASDAQ's arrangement with Reuters that promotes research of under-covered companies. Not just coverage of companies with zero or one analyst, but also coverage of the company that once had eight or nine analysts 3 years ago but now has seen coverage significantly decline. So this is definitely a way to leverage the revenue opportunity that we have and, at the same time, to also establish a consistent track record with companies as a service provider.

SELWAY: So the growth in listings business is being driven more by product?

O'BRIEN: No, I think it is a combination of the two. We see great opportunity as some of the barriers have come down. Companies that might not have previously evaluated any listing market, NASDAQ notwithstanding, are starting to realize that they have options that they should evaluate.

SELWAY: Noreen, how about the exchange?

CULHANE: We certainly routinely reach out to our listed company base, much along the same lines as Bill discussed. We constantly communicate with them about the things that they would find helpful. As NASDAQ has done, we have built a portfolio of services that largely speaks to reaching into the investor community, whether with analysts' meetings, or broad media coverage. We have 33 media entities that broadcast live from the exchange every day, and we give our listed

---

[6] NASDAQ entered into a definitive agreement to acquire Shareholder.com on Jan. 10, 2006. Shareholder.com, a privately held, Massachusetts-based firm specializing in shareholder communications and investor relations intelligence services, had over 1,000 clients at the time.

companies the opportunity to tell their stories very broadly. You met one of them earlier – Bob Pisani, who routinely looks for content for CNBC programming. Some of our other services are more targeted at specific retail and institutional audiences, both domestically and internationally. It will change for us over time here because Bill has an audience that is quite different from ours. If you look at the average company, it is about size and needs. There are large companies in both NASDAQ and the New York. But if you look across the aggregate list of companies, they are quite different. Where there are - I have heard – as many as perhaps 1,000 companies on the NASDAQ looking for analyst coverage, that number on the New York is 200. However, if you look at the Arca platform, we will be getting into the same space with NASDAQ. Looking at the opportunity to provide research to our companies, etc., particularly on that platform, will become a higher priority.

I would like to mention something our companies have approached us about. We have accommodated it rather successfully, although we have not advertised it much. That is, sitting on a customer list that has $22 trillion in market valuation, projects a very powerful voice. One of the things that John Thain has done extraordinarily well is to aim that voice in a direction that can be helpful to our listed companies. We have spent a great deal of time, for example, over the last 18 months, meeting groups of our listed companies – particularly the CFOs, chairs of audit committees, and the audit community generally – as well with the PCAOB[7] and the SEC, to focus on areas that really matter to our listed companies. Regulation is one of them. Sarbanes-Oxley, and particularly Section 404 and PCAOB Rule 2,[8] are critically important to them as they assess their ability to grow and compete on a global stage. We have done very good work on specific recommendations. John Thain, speaking for those companies, is extremely credible in Washington.

We have had several Congressmen visit us directly. John has presented to the SEC and to the PCAOB. Marshall Carter, our chairman, spoke to a congressional committee this past week. A better balance between the cost and benefit of good regulation is critical for the ability of U.S. companies to compete on a global stage. Yesterday we had the chairman of the Federal Energy Regulatory Commission. We have had Energy Secretary Samuel Bodman. We have had Al Gonzalez, our attorney general. We have had Secretary Carlos Gutierrez at the exchange, and Donald Evans when he was commerce secretary. All of these people have been at the exchange in the last several months, meeting in small intimate groups with the CEOs of our listed companies to provide both access to that community, to those key decision makers, and to listen to them very carefully in a closed door session with no media – no recording, just unfettered access.

---

[7] Public Company Accounting Oversight Board.

[8] Under Section 404 of the Sarbanes-Oxley Act of 2002, and corresponding SEC rules, certain companies in their annual reports to the agency are required to include management's evaluation of the effectiveness of companies' internal controls over financial reporting. Section 404 also requires these companies' auditors to verify and report on the internal control assessments by management.

Our listed companies tell us that this is one of the most critically important things that we provide. We will continue to focus on it. I will say also that those luminaries who visit us are from outside the exchange as well. We have had visits from Prime Minister Man Mohan Singh of India. We have had the last three leaders of China visit us.

SELWAY: This question is for John McGonegal. It seems like things have accelerated on the new product side. We now have oil ETFs. We have housing price futures, gold ETFs, and silver ETFs. Is that trend accelerating? How do both your organizations fit in?

MCGONEGAL: Yes. ETFs will morph, eventually, into asset classes, whether it is, as you mentioned, oil currencies, commodity baskets, etc. Then, probably, the next step will be actively managed ETFs, which we are in the process of working on. Right now it is kind of stuck in regulatory purgatory, as they say.

SELWAY: How long would you expect on the actively managed ETFs?

MCGONEGAL: We were hoping by the end of this year.[9] But I am not too certain. They are shaking their heads at me that it will not occur. But that is indeed where the real growth will be. They sliced and diced every sort of sector that you can imagine in the equity world. I do not know if there is any more growth left there. But it will really be on the asset class side.

SELWAY: CME?

LABUSZEWSKI: You mentioned one of my favorite pet projects, the property derivatives. Our involvement in property derivatives probably dates back about 20 years. About 18 months ago we first publicly announced our interest in developing housing futures and options, based upon the newly-re-titled S&P/Case-Shiller Home Price Indexes. We quickly received many calls from people claiming an intellectual property right. I trotted up to the 31st floor of our building where we have our archives and retrieved four or five dusty boxes, which evidenced that we had been having discussions of this nature going back to the mid-1980s. The concept is not entirely new. But the time may now be ripe.

When we turn on the news media these days, we hear talk of the housing bubble, or the housing boom. The bottom line is that while housing is not an asset class that meets the traditional criteria for the subject of a futures contract, in some other ways it is perhaps overqualified. It is overqualified in the sense that it is a huge market. According to flow of funds data from the U.S. Federal Reserve, at the conclusion of 2005 the market value of housing was something on the order of $23 trillion in the United States. That exceeds the value of domestic equities, and falls just a bit short of the value of the domestic fixed-income markets. Essentially, it is an asset class that is too big to ignore.

---

[9] Neal Wolfkoff, CEO of the Amex, said in early May 2007 that the first actively managed ETFs could be ready for launch by year-end. In a published interview, he said the Amex had issued patents for software that would make the new instruments possible. At this time, nearly all of the 500 ETFs in the U.S. were based on an index of securities that is reconstituted periodically.

I am heartened by the fact that beginning around March of 2005, an over-the-counter property derivatives market started to emerge in the United Kingdom. By some estimates, perhaps a billion sterling in commercial, and half a billion sterling in residential over-the-counter property swaps, have been traded in 2005. This trend is making its way across the pond to the United States. We hope to be at the forefront of this. We are hoping to launch this product very, very shortly.[10]

SELWAY: Let us get back to the NYSE and NASDAQ. What drives the decision to list on your exchanges? I mean, how do you compete? What is on a company's mind? Is it price? Brand? Can you give us some color on how companies make that decision?

CULHANE: As I said earlier, there are several components to that decision, Jamie. Brand is an important component. People do want to be seen listed alongside leaders in their particular space. Fundamentally, when you sit face-to-face with a CFO or a CEO, or for that matter anybody else on the management team, they are very willing to delve into the information and look closely at the full compliment of data that we present. It is not just about speed. It is also about fill rates. It is also about all the Dash 5 data.[11] It is about all the trading. It is about the full complement of trading services. There are many, many ways to slice and dice and look at things. At the end of the day people do understand their fiduciary responsibility. Listed companies absolutely want to do the right thing for their shareholders. We are very gratified that we compete most successfully.

In the IPO space, we continue to garner, as I said earlier, 90% of the qualified proceeds – 90% of the dollars raised that meet our standards. Admittedly, that is a smaller part of the pie, at only 30–35% of the pie. But we are looking to grow that on the Arca side. Companies look at the services that we can provide. They clearly look at the information that we can provide.

Here the specialist does a two-fold job. The job is not just ensuring that there is provisional liquidity introduced into the marketplace to dampen volatility. It also involves providing meaningful information. We supplement that with a dedicated client service team that is assigned to each company, as well as the team that the specialist provides. Our password-protected tools speak both to trading information and to investor information. Most recently we introduced a password-protected Website that is focused on governance. Our companies can interact with us directly on compliance with governance and our listings standards. And there are the market quality issues of the specialist's job, including lowering transaction costs. It is very important to present not just our own data, but that of respective third parties that shows the positive value of choosing to list on the NYSE.

---

[10] In late May 2006, the CME introduced contracts for the S&P/Case-Shiller Home Price indexes that track averages in 10 U.S. cities as well as an aggregate measure of the overall U.S. housing market.

[11] Dash 5 data, published monthly, comply with SEC Rule 11Ac1-5 ("Dash 5") and includes various measures of execution quality for individual securities.

SELWAY: Bill, is price a factor at all?

O'BRIEN: It is, because the process, in general, is getting a lot more rational. From a brand legitimacy perspective, that issue which has been predominant, historically, has become neutralized, or a matter of debate. One of the most telling examples was in conjunction with our 35th anniversary. We introduced a re-segmentation of our listing standards in the introduction of a NASDAQ Global Select Market.[12] This has listing standards that are not only more rigorous from a financial integrity than those of the NYSE, but that are the most rigorous in the world. The most interesting part of the Global Select Market is that there are about a thousand NASDAQ- listed companies which qualify. These are a thousand companies that not only qualify for the toughest standards in the world, but which also continue, year after year, their affiliation with NASDAQ. That is a real hallmark of the company you keep when you are in NASDAQ with these companies (not that there are not many fine companies on the NYSE that we would love to have as well!).

CULHANE: I will just point out that 86% of our list meets your new standards.

O'BRIEN: Yes, that is right. We would like to have all of them!

CULHANE: Good luck!

O'BRIEN: Noreen and I are in complete agreement on one thing – the objective criteria of performance, price and service that companies are looking at. Each account will weight those differently, especially at the higher end of the market capitalization, shares outstanding, or the disparity in fees between NASDAQ and the NYSE, which charges several hundred thousand dollars a year, versus a company on NASDAQ with fewer total shares outstanding, where it may only be ten or twenty thousand dollars. They will weigh that. They realize that they have an obligation not only to themselves but also to their investors. You can get into an argument about 74% or 72% market share all day long. But it is undeniable that the trend is for greater electronic trading, greater competition, and greater transparency in the marketplace. NASDAQ has been pioneering that for the last 35 years. When you combine that with our state of the art platform, the lowest prices in the industry, and a compelling service and product proposition, some heads are turning. It is injecting a fair dose of rationality into a process that, in the past, may have been purely image driven.

SELWAY: Let's take some questions from the audience. Bill Harts?

BILL HARTS (Banc of America Securities) [From the Floor]: I heard Noreen talk about the number of companies looking for research coverage on New York. I believe you said 200. I remember a statistic, I think it was from David Weald's National Research Exchange, that showed if you add to the number of companies that are under covered, the overall number looking for research is much higher. One

---

[12] On July 1, 2006, NASDAQ National Market was renamed NASADAQ Global Market and launched NASDAQ Global Select Market as part of this. NASDAQ Global Select was created for a segment of the newly-named Global Market with the highest initial listing standards of any exchange.

of the main things a listing company would look for from the exchange is how you could get them more, or better research coverage. I would pose the question, how would you do that?

Then for Bill, I would ask, can you give us some measurement, or some metrics, that would tell us about the success of your program to provide research for listed companies? How is it doing? How many companies have signed up? How much research has been provided?

CULHANE: We do have companies that think that they are under covered or under-served. We have companies that think that they are over served. We have companies that do not necessarily want 33 analysts covering them. It is a huge amount of work for their investor relations departments. We have companies that think that they have the right number, but not the right quality of coverage. It really comes in so many different shapes and forms. But I do think that you are right. It is really important to deliver to the investing community good information that is carefully thought through, quantitative and analytical. We see that the coverage is now shifting from the sell-side to the buy-side. We see different kinds of things happen as the economic model and the economic underpinning for research has dramatically changed. But, fundamentally, we try to get our companies access to investors by, for example, hosting conferences in Europe.

We take a group of companies to London every year. We invite them to use our facility for their own analyst meetings. And we have companies as large as Exxon Mobile doing an analyst meeting every year at the exchange, as well as very small companies like LeapFrog Technologies. We participate in the Money Show.[13] We sponsor our companies to participate to get them broader access and coverage. We are actively engaged in negotiations with a third-party provider of independent research coverage which, under the auspices of the exchange, either branded or not, or co-branded – we are not quite sure about that yet – will be offering something. It is important to really partner with somebody who has a proven product, who can get you out there with credibility.

A lot of people talk about independent research, but it has been tough sledding. We have seen many people get into it and then get out of it because of the economics. It is something that we stepped into very carefully. As I said, we have been much more aggressive of late, in preparation for the first wave of listings on the Arca platform, where we think that we really have a much more critical need in that space.

O'BRIEN: I agree with two points that Noreen made. One, you want to put the facilitation of research coverage in the broader issue of generating issuer visibility. We have institutional investor conferences overseas akin to the NYSE efforts. To do those things, we use our visibility and access (like the MarketSite) for analyst days, press events, NASDAQ.com, and our institutional investor Websites. I also agree with Noreen that building out the infrastructure for such an initiative takes time. We launched IRN a little less than a year ago. Partnering with the right independent

---

[13] The Money Show produced by InterShow of Sarasota, FL., is regularly hosted in various U.S. cities for Wall Street investors.

research providers is important. We have about 25 in the stable. It is also important, because you do not want to make a commitment to your listed companies to facilitate research and then say we can only do it in the following sectors. We want to have broad sub-industry classification coverage. We have also assembled our Research Independence Council that chooses providers for listed companies, and establishes the rules of engagement for interaction between a company and the research provider. This goes back to the question about meeting a high standard of integrity for the product. This has been a fundamental flaw in previous independent or company-funded research models.

SELWAY: Let's take some more questions from the floor.

UNIDENTIFIED SPEAKER [From the Floor]: My question starts off with the CME. Through OneChicago, you list single stock futures. Do you feel that there is any kind of cross sell there with cash equity trading? Would the CME look to become something of a JV of one of the equity exchanges? Regarding my question for the equity exchanges, there is a lot of talk about multi-asset class trading. Do you feel that single stock futures are a nexus between cash equity trading and the futures industry? Would you look to list single stock futures on your own exchanges?

LABUSZEWSKI: Our investment in OneChicago is in the form of a joint venture investment, originally with the Chicago Board Options Exchange, Chicago Board of Trade.[14] More recently, Interactive Brokers has become involved as well. I am not sure how much room there is for other investors. Then again, I am not qualified to respond to that. But I do believe that, like many other products that are traded on futures exchanges, or security futures exchanges, there are opportunities for synergies. Perhaps the most striking example of this phenomenon may be cited in the context of our Eurodollar futures contract. The Eurodollar futures are the single largest, most actively traded futures contract worldwide. There is a tremendous amount of synergy, interaction and cross-fertilization between the Eurodollar futures market and the interest rate swap markets.

The interest rate swap markets and Eurodollars were, coincidentally, rolled out at roughly the same time. The seminal IRS was transacted in 1980 and Eurodollar futures were introduced in December 1981. Originally, they were sold as sort of a tool for bank asset liability managers. There is a famous headline that we like to cite frequently at the Merc. It is, kind of, like a "Dewey defeats Truman" headline. An article appeared in a prestigious industry publication that decried the failure of the Eurodollar futures market 6 months after it was introduced. Pretty soon, interest rate swap players started to figure out that Eurodollars could be used as a pricing basis and, sort of, as a building block tool to hedge other interest rate swaps. Well, you know the rest of the story. Both markets grew to a considerable size. We have plotted out the growth.

---

[14] The Chicago Board of Trade and the ChicagoMercentile Exchange finalized their merger in a $11.9 billion transaction in July 2007. The friendly bid by the CME was accepted by shareholders of both companies. CBOT Holdings stock was de-listed and its shareholders received shares in the new company, CME Group, along with dividends.

They have both, more or less, ebbed and flowed at the same times. I do not think that is a coincidence. We believe that there are many complementary relationships to be taken advantage of between futures and other complementary products.

O'BRIEN: When our new trading platform is rolled out, hopefully by this year in December, we will look to become more aggressive in other asset classes, whether that is futures, single stock futures, and other instruments. Right now, the platform allows us to trade only two asset classes, equities and ETFs. Options will be rolled out shortly.[15] The new platform allows us to be much more aggressive. But in terms of side-by-side trading, we have seen a lot of benefits in terms of liquidity and spreads once the ETF is up and running, and the associated option is trading with it. So, we will look to be much more aggressive in those areas.

SELWAY: Sure, there are symmetries and synergies in a multi-product listings business. But is a listings business a global business?

MCGONEGAL: Yes, absolutely. I will tell a story about Tel Aviv, and you guys can jump in. We pulled into the Tel Aviv Hilton. Waiting in the lobby to check in was a team from the London Stock Exchange – their AIM group.[16] The chairman and the rest of us went to a meeting with a prospective company, and coming out of the meeting, once again, was the AIM stock market. We similarly run into the Toronto Stock Exchange on many of our calls. After all, the mineral, mining, oil and gas companies are global industries. AIM, I believe, had 12 listing meetings and seminars in North America in the last 2 months. So we have seen a lot of competition for our companies to jointly list on the London Stock Exchange, to dual list. We have had a lot of inquiries from them on whether it makes sense. Everywhere we travel we see more and more exchanges competing.

O'BRIEN: It is absolutely a global business – probably on three levels. One is where there is not a vibrant home country market. Israel would be an example. Outside of North America, the largest number of NASDAQ listings come from Israel. We are effectively their stock market by proxy. Where there is a vibrant home country exchange, then it is not a question of pursuing a U.S. or home country listing; it is a question of whether or not to list in both places. Does a U.S. listing bring incremental investor awareness, and oftentimes consumer awareness in the United States? That is where a U.S. listing, in tandem with a home country listing, may make sense. For those types of companies, attracting investor capital is less

---

[15] As of October 2007, NASDAQ Options Market seemed tentatively scheduled for launch by December 2007. Those plans were overshadowed the following month when NASDAQ formally joined the big players in options trading, agreeing to pay $652 million in cash for the Philadelphia Stock Exchange. The Philadelphia exchange is the third largest options market in the U.S. Nasdaq said the purchase would be completed in the first quarter of 2008 and it would contribute to company earnings the following year. NASDAQ launched Portal in August, an electronic platform for buying and selling private securities.

[16] AIM, or Alternative Investment Market, is the London Stock Exchange's global market for small, growing companies. Over 2,500 companies have joined AIM since it was launched in 1995, according to the exchange.

relevant. Goldman Sachs and Lehman can buy Nokia on the Finnish Exchange just as easily as they can buy it on the New York Stock Exchange.

MCGONEGAL: The flip side is that we have seen a lot of companies, about 65 or so in the last 2 years, come down from Toronto and dually list on the AMEX. Toronto is fairly illiquid. It is a smaller marketplace, and they can get access to their retail investors. I think that you will see more countries dual list in the U.S. markets if we can ever get over this Sarbanes-Oxley hurdle,[17] or if other countries start to move to a more Sarbanes-like Oxley environment.

O'BRIEN: That is the wild card when you speak of AIM. Personally, I do not view AIM as a competitor.

MCGONEGAL: Not yet.

O'BRIEN: Right, "not yet" is probably the right qualifier here. AIM is seeking not only foreign but U.S. based companies that are not yet ready for a U.S. public listing. But AIM may be more of a competitor for round C and round D venture capital financing, where those investors want some secondary market liquidity and visibility. However, the companies in this group with a poor track record are a risk in the listing business. Is that a platform that can be broadened out?

MCGONEGAL: Yes, we have even seen some U.S. companies bypass us entirely for the TSX Venture Exchange, or for listings in income trusts on the Toronto Stock Exchange.[18] These companies once again are small and, to Bill's point, private, with $100, 200, maybe 300 million in market capital. That is something which all of us on this panel should be aware of. Sarbanes-Oxley is becoming quite a hindrance for us to compete. AIM might not be a competitor now, but we have to keep it on our radar screen.

CULHANE: This is a critical question. It speaks not just to Sarbanes-Oxley, and certainly not just to small companies. It speaks to the competitiveness of the U.S. capital markets globally. We are seeing a fundamental change here that we ought to pay a lot of attention to. If you go back just 5 years and look at the non-U.S. companies that went public and raised money in the U.S. capital markets, about half of the dollars raised were in registered public offerings. The other half was raised in private placement. If you look at the capital raised this year by non-U.S. companies in the U.S. markets, only a small percent of the value was raised in registered public offerings; most of it was raised in private placements.[19] This country desperately

---

[17] One analyst, writing in March 2006, noted that until recently, a U.S. listing for Canadian companies resulted in regulatory burdens more onerous than in Canada – especially parts of the U.S. Sarbanes-Oxley law. However, Ontario, home to the Toronto Stock Exchange, had then recently introduced Sarbanes-Oxley-like regulation. Of course, the advantages of a dual listing for a Canadian company included exposure to U.S. institutional investors who would have a direct way to invest in a non-US company within the U.S. markets.

[18] The Toronto Stock Exchange and the TSX Venture Exchange are owned by the TSX Group.

[19] Culhane subsequently noted that in 2006, of the capital raised by non-U.S. companies in the U.S. markets, only eight percent of the value was raised in registered public offerings; the other 92% percent was raised in private placements.

needs tort reform. The litigation that these companies are exposed to has turned them in a different direction. Certainly, Sarbanes-Oxley is another significant factor. The reconciliation of different GAPs globally has got to be accelerated. The notion that we have companies complying with multiple sets of GAP is ludicrous. At the end of the day, the deepening home markets clearly will allow companies to raise significant dollars in their home market. The introduction of the Euro has done that for the European markets. At the end of the day, though, you just have to look as far as the China Construction Bank last year raising a billion dollars last year on the Hong Kong Stock Exchange.

The world has changed, and we really need to pay attention. It is not only about the 100 million and 200 million dollar companies. Yes, there are 29 U.S. companies listed on AIM. But that is not the only issue. We need to look at this in a much broader perspective. We need to pay a lot of attention, or else an area where the U.S. markets have always been number one is in jeopardy.

SELWAY: Noreen, is this a driver for exchange consolidation globally?

CULHANE: I am happily in a quiet period.

SELWAY: Oh. Anyone else who is not in a quiet period feel like answering…

LABUSZEWSKI: I am not in a quiet period. Fortunately, I can say that the globalization of the futures markets is not being driven or constrained by Sarbanes-Oxley.

SELWAY: Not yet.

LABUSZEWSKI: The availability of electronic trading platforms is what is driving the globalization of the futures markets. It was not too many years ago when trading was confined to a pit environment during U.S. trading hours. Under those circumstances, even though we may have offered many products that had international appeal, it was difficult to get traders in other nations involved. That is no longer the case. Our Globex electronic trading platform has an international reach. We operate it virtually 24 h a day. We have six international hubs: Dublin, London, Paris, Gibraltor, Amsterdam and Singapore. We are also in Asia with hubs that provide convenient access to our system. Frankly, because of our electronic trading platform that is coupled with some outreach programs, we have seen some European and Asian incentive programs featuring discounted exchange fees. We have seen a tremendous increase in our volume coming from overseas. We have actually focused many of our new product efforts on the development of international products.

SELWAY: We have one last question from our host, and then we will break for lunch.

SCHWARTZ: The listing decision is a very important one, and a very important dimension of inter-market, inter-exchange competition. I would like to ask if you could say a word or two about how vibrant this source of competition will remain in the future. There are any number of things that can impact it. Sarbanes-Oxley is one. Unlisted trading privileges is another. I even wonder about the sophistication of the listed companies concerning the market structure issues that we talk about here. I was struck earlier when you, Noreen, and Bill were talking about the transparency of markets, volatility, and trading costs. If I am not mistaken, five or

10 years ago that would not even have been mentioned, because the listed companies were not tuned into these measures of market quality. In this context, can you say a word about the vibrancy of competition going forward?

O'BRIEN: My frame of reference is my background in trading from my time as COO of Brut.[20] I can tell you that the competition in the market for a listing, at least today, is just as much, if not even more rough and tumble, than the competition for order flow among exchanges and among brokers. You are right. People today are more focused on what the core issues are. Historical perceptions of the listing decision, in general, have faded away. The right criteria to evaluate your listing decision have really become much more objective. What that means is a rigorous and regular evaluation of your listing market and whether or not it makes sense for your investors.

CULHANE: I agree with Bill. Listings will continue to be very competitive. It is a major source of revenue for the exchanges, one of the key ones. We applaud the notion of choice. We think that the U.S. markets are the strongest capital markets in the world. All of them are really good markets. This is not about black hats and white hats, or good guys and bad guys. This is, fundamentally, about lots of good choice. But at the end of the day, to your point on UTP trading, one of the critical things that an exchange provides, particularly as an SRO, is to support the SEC's goal of protecting investors. You must have a listed market, and there must be listing standards. You have to comply with the listing standards. Those are financial and governance related standards. You have to have a place where there is a look at the ultimate investor, protecting that investor, and giving investors some sense of comfort should they chose to invest in one of the companies listed on your exchange.

You certainly cannot say that shares will be going go up or down. But you can say that they meet the standards that have been set with a lot of careful thought toward the notion of truly providing investors fair access to good companies. Transparency is key. Choice is key. At the end of the day, our issuers do a very rigorous exercise in terms of looking at the markets. We would like to acknowledge that yes, there have been a couple of companies recently that left the New York for NASDAQ. There have also been 92 companies over the last 5 years that have come the other way. It is good healthy competition.

Once you get complacent you get sloppy. Having strong competitors makes us all that much better. In the end, that serves the issuer and, ultimately, the shareholder.

SELWAY: I would add that, when NASDAQ begins listing, one and two and three symbol tickers next January, things will get real interesting, real competitive, and potentially a little confusing.[21]

Please join me in thanking the panel.

---

[20] William O'Brien subsequently joined Direct Edge ECN at Knight Capital Group as CEO on July 2007 from NASDAQ. He joined NASDAQ as part of its 2004 acquisition of BRUT ECN, where he was senior vice president, new listings, at the time of the conference.

[21] The SEC approved a plan in July 2007 that permits NYSE listed companies to keep their three-letter ticker symbols if they transfer to NASDAQ, which uses four or five letters for its companies. As envisaged, the new rule would not allow NASDAQ to list new companies with three letter tickers.

Chapter 5
Emergence of New Competition: Alternative Sources of Liquidity

William Harts, Alfred Berkeley, Luca Filippa, James Ross,
George Sofianos, Larry Tabb, and Mark Wright

WILLIAM HARTS: I would like to welcome everyone to our panel discussion. The topic is Emergence of New Competition: Alternative Sources of Liquidity. That the past few years have seen a tremendous increase in the number of alternative equity trading venues is no surprise to most people in this room. It is also no surprise that we have seen relentless and sometimes brutal competition in this space. It has led to the failure or consolidation of many of the new participants. Our panel will explore the dynamics behind this competition, the causes and nature of it, and what we anticipate going forward.

The people on this panel represent, either as operators or analysts, some of the best liquidity sources that have been developed to date. I will quickly introduce them. Starting on my left is Al Berkeley, Chairman of Pipeline Trading Systems. Next to Al is Luca Filippa, Director of Research and Development for Borsa Italiana. Jim Ross, who many of you know as one of the original developers and operators of Instinet Crossing, is currently CEO of Matchpoint Trading. We also have George Sofianos who is responsible for Equity Execution Strategies at Goldman Sachs; Larry Tabb, CEO of Tabb Group, which writes a lot of insightful analysis in this space; and, finally, Mark Wright, Managing Director of Global Product Management at ITG.

Let's jump into some questions for the panel. I encourage people in the audience to raise their hands if they want to add something or ask additional questions. People in the industry talk a lot about what the differentiating features are of a particular trading system or alternative liquidity source. How important is that differentiator in the success of a new trading operation? Do you need to come up with a better way of trading, a silver bullet, so to speak, or a better mousetrap? Or, can you compete on the surface? Is it some combination of the two approaches? Can you compete on price? What are the differentiators? I am opening this up to the entire panel. Al, do you want to start?

ALFRED BERKELEY: Sure. You need an offering that really makes a difference. You must have a value proposition that is not otherwise being filled. I can tell you a bit about the value proposition that we think makes sense for Pipeline, which many of you know has been in business for about 18 months. We have been trying to expand and recreate the institutional block market. This market had been severely

R.A. Schwartz et al. (eds.), *Competition in a Consolidating Environment*,
doi: 10.1007/978-0-387-75943-2_5, © Springer Science+Business Media, LLC 2008

impacted by decimalization and the growth of predatory algorithms. We thought there was an opportunity to expand and recreate this market, working with the other people who are trying to recreate the block. We thought the value added we could offer would be really large block sizes, a secure environment in which to trade, and high quality executions.

We have attacked three specific problems: the disincentive to go first; the disincentive to put your true price in place; and the disincentive to put your true size in place. Those three problems in the existing markets, we thought, would allow us to participate in the recreation of the block market. Today, we are up to about 400 institutional customers, which is pretty far ahead in our plan. We are real happy with our value proposition. I would say it is our response to the problem that the customer is trying to solve that has given Pipeline an opportunity to create a new business. It has to start with the customer's pain.

GEORGE SOFIANOS: It is fairly obvious that we all need to differentiate from each other because the field is crowded. Differentiation going forward is absolutely essential. At Goldman, we are planning to differentiate ourselves by leveraging our full range of execution platforms. Whatever execution serves the clients' needs, we will provide. Low touch in the execution venues: REDIPlus provides that low touch and is rolling out its new SIGMA X smart router, aggregating both displayed and non-displayed liquidity. We also have for portfolio trading, high-touch agency executions. Finally, there is the jewel in the crown, leveraging Goldman Sachs' famed risk appetite by providing capital to clients for the very large, very difficult trades.

MARK WRIGHT: Our primary system is POSIT. We have been around so long I am not sure we qualify as an alternative any more. We are coming up on our 20th anniversary. We started out very much in the confidentiality end of the space. That was a key motivator – zero information leakage and high quality mid-point prints. Over the years we have continued to enhance that. As our clients' needs have changed, the technology has gotten better, so we now can do continuous crossing. As trading desks have increasingly wanted to manage cash and risk, we have added cash and risk management features.

Over the years, there has been an evolution with the clients' interests. The number one differentiator that we all agree on is liquidity. If you are building some kind of alternative liquidity pool, and if you want to convince people to come, you had better get some results. It is clear, going forward, that people have become comfortable giving up a bit more information to attract liquidity. We are starting to move in response to that as well. We are doing things in our indications of interest matching with our POSIT Alert product.

JAMES ROSS: I am very much a start-up. I had the pleasure of competing with ITG over the years in the 1980s and 1990s, having spent quite a bit of time at Instinet's Crossing system. You get a certain benefit from having the infrastructure and the support surrounding you in that world. What I have been observing, especially as I started a new business, are the needs of the clients. I look at where I want to place my business and take advantage of what is currently available. Reg. ATS has given us an opportunity to get into the game without incurring a huge regulatory burden.

That has been very beneficial to a small start-up like mine given that we have a system and are looking for the right place to expand. That is true for the exchange pilot as well as for the broker/dealer ATSs.

The opportunities and the value propositions of the exchange products that will be offered, for example, and the value propositions of the broker/dealers (BDs) and the bulge-bracket BDs, will be quite different. We have to be selective and specific. I cannot possibly compete when ITG is offering multiple value propositions in different areas of transaction research, in crossing, portfolio management, or just basic trading.

The way I look at it is, how will a call market offering apply and fit into this very rapidly evolving environment? Certainly exchanges are an option, the BD with internalization is an option, and then also, let us just call it a crossing only kind of a facility, is an option. We feel that we have a value proposition that can morph with any particular venue. That is one of the good things about being a start-up. MatchPoint is not a stand-alone business. It is designed with a partner, or acquirer in mind.[1]

The barriers to entry and survival are very high in this fiercely competitive industry. Building redundant corporate infrastructure and connectivity brings no value to our business model. On the contrary, they drain valuable resources and capital away from our primary focus. As a result, we concentrate on point-in-time, benchmark matching with the idea of making it attractive – almost like a "plug-in" – to the independent ATSs, bulge bracket firms, and exchanges. These have the corporate infrastructure and connectivity in place.

MatchPoint prospects potential partners based on its primary strength, our matching platform, and courts multiple opportunities. Being a start-up, MatchPoint can identify the best approach for success without the burden of legacy business commitments and operational limitations.

HARTS: What I am hearing is that it helps to have a silver bullet if you want to attract that liquidity, at least initially. Over time it might evolve into a more service-based model. As Mark pointed out, at one time POSIT was the new kid on the block. The system that had clear differentiation from anything else that was out there. Over the nearly 20 years that it has been in operation, there have been many other systems that have tried to make a dent in its market share. I would say that most have failed, and that it is very difficult to compete in this area. Earlier we heard that the ISE is going into this same area. We will see what the key to success is there.

With the combination of cheaper technology and a more favorable regulatory environment, have we evolved to where it is easier to start a new liquidity source or an alternative trading system? Is it easier, or harder, to get to where you need to be to start one of these system?

LARRY TABB: Yes (laughter). You are right on both counts. First, from a technology standpoint, there is more off-the-shelf technology that you can use to build these

---

[1] NYSE Group acquired MatchPoint Trading in July 2006.

systems, to create matching technologies, algorithms and technology products. It is much easier today for broker/dealers to go out and buy this non-proprietary technology and to create their own matching engines and ATSs. On the flip side, the amount of noise out there, and the ability to get your platform on a desk and actually used, is now a lot harder.

It is not like it was years ago when ITG started up and said, "Look, I am doing this electronically, and there are all these guys out there charging you a lot, so we will charge you a little less, and it will be electronic, streamlined and neat." Now, everybody on the block has a cool, neat tool that does something a little bit differently than everyone else. The problem is that, on both the buy-side and sell-side desks, how many platforms can you have? How many different algorithms can you understand and use, and know how they interact with your flow?

The problem is not can I build a better mousetrap, but can I distribute and create a value proposition around that mousetrap. The technology part is much easier and cheaper. The problem of getting it out to the market is much harder. It is tremendously overwhelming in this day and age.

HARTS: The distribution point is a good one. A few years ago Instinet had a tremendous number of sell-side traders' desks, and that was a monopoly situation for them. Over time, as more platforms were rolled out with broker/dealers sponsoring, for instance (can I get in a plug here just to be fair [laughter]?) Banc of America's InstaQuote platform, and Goldman's REDIPlus platform, the hope, at one time, was that windows-based technology would make it easier to get a lot of these on a single desktop. But it does not seem to have happened that way.

TABB: It is easier to get the stuff on the desktop. The problem is how many systems can someone learn to use? Plus, even though it is less expensive to put it on someone's desktop, it still needs a FIX connection.[2] It has to be tested, it has to be integrated. For that matter, something that one of these guys on the table gives to someone for free is still not free when someone on the buy-side has to actually use it.

ROSS: Yes, and I would take that one step further: The institutional frustration is not just with order fragmentation, but with system fragmentation. They have gotten so many systems coming at them with the newest, hottest, DMA, OMS, crossing network, what have you. So get in line for the broker approval process. At MatchPoint we decided to focus singularly on developing and specializing in the call market (the crossing venue), as opposed to building the infrastructure. I could never compete with a Credit Suisse, or an exchange, or anything like that. At the same time, I cannot wait for the institutional broker approval process to let me finally start doing business.

The reality, interestingly enough, of being able to offer a new product is that, without question, you have to rely on a strategic partner, or set of partners. Even

---

[2] FIX, or Financial Information Exchange, is the standard electronic protocol for pre-trade communications and trade execution introduced in the early 1990s.

ISE has brought in some additional partners, and look at the exchanges. They have people now starting to strategically position with them as well. It is not just with MatchPoint. It is true across the board with new products and services.

WRIGHT: Let me amplify that point. For all of the EMS vendors, the story of the year is that people do not want more than one or two of them. They want them to be broker neutral or multi-broker, and to access all these systems and algorithms, etc. If you had asked me 3 years ago if we would support third-party broker algorithms from our Triton product, I never would have imagined it would happen. Now it is an essential part of getting that desktop real estate.

Granted, we kind of drank the cool aid when we moved into the OMS space with our purchase of Macgregor.[3] If we had any hesitation about broker neutrality whatsoever before this purchase, we certainly had no hesitation afterwards. We have had to get used to being both completely broker neutral and open, and this is just an outgrowth of that.

On the backend, all of the alternative liquidity sources tend to have relatively low hit rates, because you cannot know what is in there. You cannot see what you are trying to trade against. So ATS aggregation is a hot technology right now, just as 5 years ago it was ECN aggregation across the visible ECN pools. As the ECNs have consolidated, those problems have been minimized, but in the ATS space it is a huge business opportunity.

BERKELEY: I would build on the comment about neutrality. At Pipeline, we are profoundly neutral. We look at channels to market, and at real estate on the desk, and we try to make it happen any way the customer wants it. That is what has allowed us to be so far ahead of plan in getting on desks. We do not fight for a particular way to get there. If the customer wants to come in through REDI, or Bloomberg, or Sonic, or any system they want – ITG, for instance, brings us a lot of orders – we want to be profoundly neutral on that issue.

HARTS: The big question is, will this happen in Europe? Let's get our friend from Borsa Italiana in here. Right now, in Italy and in Europe, it is pretty centralized.

LUCA FILIPPA: The situation in Europe is quite different. The kind of fragmentation that we have is due to the fact that the liquidity of shares is concentrated in the domestic markets – that is, in the country of incorporation of each listed company. In that sense, the London Stock Exchange is the best market for U.K. shares, Deutsche Börse for German shares, Euronext for Belgian shares, and so on. Therefore, a market participant interested in trading in the European blue chips has to look at quite a large number of markets.

In such a framework, one of the problems exchanges have to face is the need for large players to reduce the number of trading platforms they have to deal with. Of course, regulation also matters, although I do not want to go into MiFID at this

---

[3] ITG, in July 2005, announced its plan to acquire Macgregor, an OMS to the buy-side community which then had a reported 110 major institutional clients with assets of some $5.5 trillion. The acquisition was completed on January 3, 2006.

point. Exchanges have at least three areas to look at. They are represented by the needs of intermediaries, institutional investors, and retail investors. In my opinion, exchanges should always remember that they can be successful if they exploit their network capability, and ability to create and distribute network externalities.

When talking about intermediaries and any other trading members, the most important choice we have to make now is the decision about the new trading platform. At this moment, exchanges have to think carefully about one thing: should they deliver a new trading platform that will be very simple, very cheap, and very fast, while leaving the complexity and the intelligence tools to intermediaries? Or, should they try to develop a trading platform that incorporates features like portfolio insurance, stop-loss orders, algorithmic trading, and so on? I believe this is a crucial choice because it will impinge upon the competitive relationship between intermediaries and investors. It will create in some cases a level playing field. It will also increase the probability of conflicts. Careful consideration and consultation should be given to this.

When we talk to institutional investors from the fastest growing areas of business in Europe, the question of direct access arises in the sense of direct membership. Direct access to one exchange's trading system could be possible after MiFID, even if on a practical basis it is already be in place. You could have institutional investors using a proprietary link to the central trading platform through an intermediary that basically allows the investors to trade on the exchange, even if formally the responsibility still belongs to the trading member and not to the investors.

Apart from that technical point, the role exchanges in Europe and elsewhere play in providing not only trading/matching services but also new information services will be important. In that case, if the exchanges keep the liquidity in the order book, they will be able to provide a unique flow of information for a sophisticated investor about the aggregated pre-trade conditions, and also analysis about the potential impact of trades on the book. Another point when dealing with institutional investors is the possibility of block trading facilities, starting with the strong liquidity and the information flows that exchanges everywhere may count on delivering.

The last point is probably a peculiarity in Italy at the moment, but important nevertheless to all markets, the U.S. included. It concerns the role of retail investors. Changes in technology and regulation have allowed a small number of people to trade directly on exchanges with, of course, the inter-positioning of intermediaries. In Italy, we have thousands of retail investors who daily are connected with the stock market, interacting with the order book. They represent some 30% of the total number of trades. It is an important phenomenon that was also successfully adapted by some trading members who developed specific services for them. Also, for these people, it will be beneficial for the exchanges to extend the scope and the list of the securities we trade. You have already talked about ETFs. In Europe, another interesting area is that of securitized derivatives, such as covered warrants or certificates. This is an area in which some exchanges in continental Europe have been able to offer securities which incorporate a risk-return profile that is not directly tradable, or that would be tradable only at very high cost. Just think of the Chinese or Indian stock market.

HARTS: Luca, do investors and exchanges in Italy look at the competition that we have had here in the U.S. among alternative trading systems as a positive development, or does the fragmentation seem to you to be a negative?

FILIPPA: We always look at competition as a key and stable element of our business. We work in the market, so we have to face it. I must say I found the answer earlier by Noreen Culhane from the NYSE about the competition with NASDAQ very fair and interesting. Currently, in Italy at least, we are interested in the impact of regulation. It is one of the two drivers of competition. The other is IT development. The point is that we should be sure that regulatory changes always look at enhancing competition and efficiency, and that they do not provide advantages to only one part of the market.

HARTS: Does anyone else want to talk about the international aspect? I keep asking myself the question, what really would need to happen in Europe to open the gates to full competition? Will MiFID do that, in your opinion? Is it just a matter of time before there is nothing broken that needs to be fixed?

FILIPPA: I remember when the Exchanges of the 11 European countries that were adopting the euro as national currency decided as a group to start trading in euros. This was on January 4, 1999, 3 years before euro notes and coins were actually in circulation. It was the first area that enabled European citizens to become familiar with the euro. Most analysts and experts would have expected a faster consolidation of the order flow and of the exchange business because of this change. But it did not happen. Why? Competition in the provision of trading services (trading in euros, for example) – is probably the most visible element of the business, but we should not ignore the cost and the procedures in another area – post-trading clearing and settlement. As most traders may easily explain, the bulk of the cost is in the post-trading phase, not in the trading phase. However, once the consolidation now occurring among the European exchange industry is completed (let us say in 2 years time), the next step will be to set up a market for Pan-European blue chips.

As I said before, all European equity markets are highly concentrated at the domestic level. I would say that the 50 or 100 most liquid shares of stock of each domestic market accounts for more than 60–70% of the total trading volume. Therefore, with only 300–400 stocks, you could create a trading environment that would collect around two-thirds of trading and post-trading revenues of the overall industry. That will be the next area of competition. In my opinion, it is only a matter of time.

HARTS: If anyone wants to ask questions, just raise your hand and we will bring you a microphone. In the meantime, let me throw out one more question. A lot of people talk about whether or not it is advantageous or appropriate for a broker-dealer to own, or to be affiliated with an ATS or any liquidity pool. The question is, does that put the ATS at a competitive disadvantage? Are there perceived conflicts of interest from customers for ATSs that are affiliated with broker/dealers, or ECNs, or whatever, in terms of issues such as information leakage that a non-affiliated ATS or an exchange may not have to deal with? I guess this is a question for Al and Mark, maybe the two different sides of the question.

WRIGHT: It is essential that you be independent or unconflicted with respect to your trading interest. We like to say that it is in our DNA, that we are a confidential environment that we are unconflicted in our trading interests because the amount of information submitted into our crossing system is so immense. We have launched products like post-trade analysis systems that have massive amounts of information in them. People would not trust us with the information if we had any conflict of interest as we move forward into other parts of the space, like the matching of interests where you are sweeping a lot of information. It is just too important. I do not think that we could be launching certain products if we had any other proprietary trading operations. I certainly do not think that this sort of joint venture which we announced recently with Merrill Lynch[4] would have been possible if we had not been able to act as a neutral independent third party.

BERKELEY: Our core strategy, as I said earlier, is to be profoundly neutral, that is profoundly confidential. That being said, I do not think, from a public policy point of view, that it hurts the country or the overall market (the market that is increasingly electronically interconnected) to have many different models competing with each other. There are a lot of pros and a lot of cons to having integrated services if you are from a full-service broker-dealer.

What have we done in our software? We have programmed one solution to the mathematical problem known as the prisoner's dilemma. It is all about being a completely confidential, trusted agent. We happened to have put all of those rules into software, but that is the essence of being a good broker – a confidential trusted agent.

It is perfectly natural for the large broker/dealers to add electronic versions of that trusted agency to their offerings. It is part of a vibrant shifting of paradigms that you are seeing as more and more shares go through essentially closed books, blind books, totally confidential books. That is the big story that is going on beneath the surface. There is a reason why so many people are now offering electronic blind books. It is because of the problems that have arisen from the open books that have been our traditional system in the United States.

HARTS: Well, George?

SOFIANOS: Here is a broker/dealer prospective. As I mentioned, our objective at Goldman is to provide clients the full spectrum of execution choices. Of course, this runs straight into this issue of the broker/dealer conflicted priorities. It is interesting how we approached it at Goldman. We created two completely separate registered broker/dealer entities: GSCO, which is the traditional broker/dealer, and GSEC, Goldman Sachs Execution and Clearing, an agency-only broker/dealer. We housed our REDI platform and the SIGMA X Smart Router in GSEC, our agency broker/dealer. The discussions we had with our clients, and the feedback from them with the evolution of SIGMA X Smart Router, are interesting. The bottom line is

[4]On August 16, 2006, ITG entered into a 50% percent joint venture with Merrill to form Block Alert LLC., a global block order crossing service.

that we are dealing with this issue of broker/dealer order flow versus the true agency order flow, by providing clients with a choice. They can go through GSEC, or through GSCO. SIGMA X essentially tries to enhance our traditional SIGMA Smart Router that aggregated the displayed pools of liquidity by bringing in non-displayed pools of liquidity.

We have no problem convincing our clients that it is beneficial for them to bring in crossing networks like Liquidnet, for example, or some of the other automated market makers out there. But we had a long debate with our clients about whether we should allow the SIGMA X Smart Router, on the GSEC side, to interact with the big pool of liquidity in the GSCO site. That is where our clients had some ambivalence. Some of them are comfortable, and some are not. We resolved this problem by giving our clients an opt-out option, either of their own or on a trade-by-trade basis. Yes, you can use SIGMA X and, if you want, you can opt out from interacting with the GSCO pool of liquidity.

HARTS: I expect that the next panel, which includes people from the buy-side, well get deeper into this question. But it seems interesting to me that, for a long time, the buy-side has been insisting on more anonymity. They do not want their orders disclosed to a broker, if possible. Now it seems that maybe the industry has gotten over that a little bit. What I am hearing is, if you set up the appropriate walls, the information barriers, and so on, then customers – the buy-side – will trust that you will not look at their orders. It seems like we have come a long way in the industry. Yes, Jim?

ROSS: With regard to broker/dealer neutrality, the issue of capital commitment and keeping the order flow segregated is the most obvious consideration. ITG, Instinet and a lot of other agency brokers have been touting that for a long time. But there is an aspect of neutrality that involves the diversification of services and offerings by various broker/dealers actually precluding themselves from necessarily interacting with each other. As I have discovered from my years at Instinet, and certainly my time with MatchPoint, there is a certain unwillingness between competitors (bulge bracket firms and institutions alike) to interact directly with each other. If I may be blunt, I do not see Merrill's program desk sending something to Goldman Sachs's program desk to see what they execute. I may be wrong, it is just a thought.

Another really important aspect is who is bringing all of these other people together? Who is the other neutral agent who will bring together all of these bulge bracket firms that are definitely internalizing, and who also have their own proprietary books? From a crossing perspective, from a call market perspective, from a point in time matching rather than a continuous perspective, there is a lot of value in offering a call in that sense. Pipeline has done something to that degree as well. It is offering it to both sides, institutional and broker/dealer.

But let's get back to neutrality. All of the brokers are competing with each other. In this area, the independent, smaller group of ATS providers on the panel can really stand out. MatchPoint, for example, specializes in point in-time, benchmark matching. As a business, the independent ATS does not compete with the traditional business of a broker/dealer like sales trading, research, or investment banking.

Furthermore, all the ATSs embrace an agency business model, which enhances their neutrality with the buy-side and sell-side.

HARTS: Tim Riley has a question.

RILEY: Larry, you were the first one on the panel to start talking about the buy-side experience. Right now, several ATSs are represented on the panel, and the exchange, in addition to proprietary products, is also going to launch some more trading systems. You talked about the broker/dealer internal crossing engines. How does this all play out? What is the end game? If Goldman is going to do 10% of the flow, if everybody else is going to capture five to 10% or more, and the exchanges capture another 30–40%, what does this mean for a client who wants, for example, to sell a million shares of Symantec? What will happen?

TABB: That is a really good question. You hit it right on the head. Everybody is competing with everybody. The exchanges are putting algorithms in the matching engines, you have crossing networks and dark pools. You have liquidity scattered here and there. Even for sell-side firms, it will be increasingly difficult to find the other side of the transaction without something out there electronic hunting, seeking, gathering and collecting shares on the other side. We see that happening now. Where we are heading, a mess exists. Displayed liquidity is fragmented across the major market centers, regional exchanges and ECNs, while invisible liquidity is fragmented further. There are 40-plus crossing networks, dark pools, call markets. It is even hosted on exchanges, ECNs such as BATs, and so on.

UNIDENTIFIED SPEAKER: It is called OnTrade, Larry.[5]

TABB: On the exchange front you have Reg NMS increasing the amount of flow to regional exchanges like Cincinnati, Philadelphia, Boston, Pacific, Chicago, Arca and the American Stock Exchange. In addition, the Reg NMS top of book protection rules are changing behavior, making institutions think, "well, my order is not top of book on a listed-protected exchange, let me cancel and put it someplace else where it is protected." The days of being able to take a look at a market and say I want to be here at this price point – just put me there – are gone. We are moving into a new realm where algorithms, DMA, and Smart Order Routing will basically take care of it. Anybody who thinks that they have a proprietary hosted pool of liquidity that will stay there has been smoking something that I would like to have. It is all in the engines. The engines will determine where the liquidity is, where the best price is, and where I can be at the top of the book.

What do I want to do with this order? How aggressive do I want to be? Dial it in, hit the button and go. It will be very difficult to do it any other way except that the alternative liquidity pools, such as Liquidnet, Pipeline and maybe BIDs[6] ill

---

[5] OnTrade, formerly known as NextTrade ECN, is the ECN that was acquired by Citigroup in early 2006 from NextTrade Holdings.

[6] BIDS, an acronym for U.S.-based ATS, Block Interest Discovery Service, was announced in 2006. It was formed from a consortium of 12 brokerage firms including Bank of America, Credit Suisse and Goldman Sachs. During one1 week in July, for example, it reported more than 20 million shares (double counted) in executed daily volume.

have some more sticky liquidity because they just focus on matching larger blocks. But the list of venues where liquidity can be found will increase, and finding liquidity without the aid of technology will become increasingly difficult.

HARTS: Another question out there?

BROOKE ALLEN (Maple Securities)[7] [From the Floor]: You asked the first half of my question already, where is it going? The market really seems these days to be in the input parameters to all these algorithms. At the last conference I was at someone had counted 150-plus vendors with commercial algorithms and untold proprietary ones. We need to get those input parameters to find each other efficiently, without duking it out in the markets and leaving their droppings all over these little tiny trades. How do we get to that? This morning we talked about the exchanges consolidating. Wouldn't this be a natural monopoly? Let us just have a book of all the input parameters so that we can find each other and trade.

TABB: That is what is happening. Perhaps the exchange consolidation is somewhere else, but it is not happening here.

ALLEN [From the Floor]: There is one characteristic that you offer that the exchange does not. It is that I can send my trading desire to an algorithm. My specific question is about keeping things dark – is that where we are headed?

TABB: The first question Bill asked was, "Is there a silver bullet?" I do not know if anybody on this panel really answered that. The answer is "No, there is no silver bullet." You have the brokers who want to internalize. You have the exchanges that want to create either displayed or dark matching mechanisms. You have different dark pools, different light pools, and different algorithms. You have different buyers and sellers with their different needs, such as market makers, agency traders, proprietary traders, hedge funds, and individuals who all have different trading styles and needs. We have almost come down to actually anti-exchanges where there are smart algorithms looking around trying to find the other side.

Algorithms are very efficient. Even though they break up blocks into much smaller pieces, they can cycle around liquidity venues very quickly. When you have these ECNs and ATSs that are reacting sub-second, and sub-microsecond, you are not taking up much overhead. Having a fragmented liquidity environment is not really hurting us.

UNIDENTIFED SPEAKER: Also, some people have speculated about exchanges that could actually host algorithms themselves. This may be closer to what you are thinking of. There has been some development in that area and perhaps Luca was talking about something like that earlier in Italy. Yes, that might be the next iteration.

SOFIANOS: Let me take a stab at this issue. Clearly, the ideal scenario for the buy-side is for the naturals to meet with no intermediation at the higher level so that they do not go through the slicing and dicing process. That, however, is

---

[7] At the time of the conference, Mr. Allen was with MANE Fund Management, Inc.

fundamentally very difficult to achieve because severe adverse information and selection problems are involved.

Let us look at some statistics. What is the crossing networks' market share? My best guess is that the collective market share of trading volume is about 3% of trading volume. Mark put it out earlier that the hit rate is very low on his crossing network. Let us assume that it is 10% of the liquidity. Three percent market share and a 10% hit rate means there is 30% of the liquidity sitting in this system. Nobody has of yet solved the problem of how to access this 30% of liquidity that sits in the systems and somehow does not interact. That is the big challenge. Efforts like SIGMA X would certainly help, but I do not believe that we will ever be in a situation where that is the way that we trade. The way we are going is bifurcated. We will have the naturals bidding for a small percentage. I do not know what it will be, 5–15%. On the other side you will have the smart algorithms slicing out the orders, taking advantage of technology, and executing the orders efficiently over time.

ALLEN [From the Floor]: I am not proposing that an exchange host an algorithm for me. But perhaps an exchange could allow me to enter an order that nobody sees, just like I can enter an order into one of these algorithms. Nobody sees it until it shows up on the other side and we trade. That is what I mean about being dark. The structure right now dis-incents me to let anybody know. If I let somebody know that I exist, there might be some negligible advertising value, but I have written a huge option to all the people who want to front run me. I would like to say that I am there, in my size, and have nobody know. We now have the technology and we do not even need a specialist.

HARTS: By the way, just in case anyone missed it, it sounds like Goldman has a new Smart Order Router. Mark, did you want to say something?

WRIGHT: We actually have a system, an algorithm, that is attempting to address some of these issues. This is an area that will evolve dramatically over the years. Clients who are looking for passive participation in the market for their order could submit it to ITG's DarkServer algorithm. The customer decides which liquidity pools he or she wants to access. The DarkServer would then route the order out to all of these venues. The shares are never displayed in the market and orders are executed at the midpoint, or better. With this one application, we will get you to all of the ATSs in the market, to all the liquidity pools.

But here are examples of some problems that it will take years to shake out. We will bring a client order in and put it in one particular ATS. Then the client will find out, for example, that in that ATS, their order is exposed to market bound flow. Or, the order is displayed in an Alerts Window in another ATS. There are numerous nuances and features in the various ATSs that the order is exposed to. To understand and explain them all to customers is a massive educational challenge. Reaching out to all the ATSs is also a technical challenge, which we have successfully handled.

BERKELEY: I would like to address that too. Remaining hidden is at the heart of the problem that we have tried to solve. You will remember I said that we have worked on three areas of pain: (1) the disincentive that exists in the traditional exchanges, and the ECNs for going first; (2) the disincentive for showing your true price; and (3) the disincentive for showing your true size. We have very different fill rates, depending on the behavior of the people who come into Pipeline. The ones who avoid the ships crossing in the night are the ones who sit there.

We have some substantial (25%, 30%, 40%) fill rates for some clients who enter in the morning and let their large orders sit with exposure to all of the algorithms and other sources that are bringing us orders. We do not send orders out,[8] but we allow orders to come in. They get extraordinarily good fill rates. Near the end of the regular trading day, say 3:30 p.m., customers who are concerned because they still need to get that million and a half share block executed will begin using other methods to get that accomplished, such as order slicing on ATSs, or dealer capital.

That is a sort of hybrid approach to staying dark, staying big, not missing ships crossing in the night, and still having the flexibility to go to the other venues if they want. All during the morning, investors bring orders to many of our partners – (ITG, REDI, Sonic, whoever it might be) and they ping them around the Street. We sit there being pinged, but most of those orders are not big enough to cross with us, and they just fall off to the bottom.

UNIDENTIFIED SPEAKER: These emerging alternative trading systems do not provide price discovery. They depend on a strong central marketplace to conduct a match. Is there not a limit to how much they can do and still operate as a liquidity pool?

HARTS: Of course. George?

SOFIANOS: Yes, that is a very interesting question. Whenever I lose sleep over that question, I put myself back to sleep by remembering the past 5 years at the NASDAQ market when there was not (until recently with the consolidation) a centralized pool of liquidity. There is no particularly strong evidence that price discovery suffered in that market. Information technology has evolved to the extent that they now display the liquidity and the fragmented pools are connected with smart routers.

UNIDENTIFIED SPEAKER: There is a distinct difference between a retail market and a wholesale market. There is solid price discovery in the retail market, and we use that to set midpoint reference prices at which to cross our blocks.

HARTS: Yes?

ANTHONY FORTUNATO (Instinet, LLC)[9] [From the Floor]: Al made a great point. He spoke about resting liquidity that gets paid but does not execute because the size is not large enough. Do you think that the solution to your problem is to educate the buy-side more to actually trade in blocks, and to complain less that

---

[8] In April 2007, Pipeline said it had developed an Algorithm Switching Engine that is able to predict the performance of third-party algorithmic trading strategies. The idea is to offer these algorithms to traders while they are waiting for a match in the block marketplace. The product was launched in November 2007.

[9] At the time of the conference, Mr. Fortunato was Director of U.S. Equity Sales and Trading at Nomura Securities International.

there is no place to trade blocks? I would argue that the NASDAQ or ECN market-place is the largest hidden pool of liquidity if people want to use it. Display a hundred behind it, but if people are pinging they will realize that somebody else is there. How do you solve that?

BERKELEY: We think this is a normal market maturation issue. We think that our customers are generally smart. We now have enough of them who have figured this out and have begun to add substantial liquidity in some stocks by having these big blocks sitting there. It is as much word of mouth, and confidence. You need to build confidence that these big blocks will trade at the right prices. We do not see how you can force that. We do not see how to hurry that. We believe that this will come with time, and all the signs are that it is coming our way.

HARTS: Isn't what you are describing part of a bigger problem? I mean, bench-marks are chosen. They can be established by portfolio managers, or plan sponsors, or consultants. The decision of whether or not to trade VWAP versus getting it done at all may be out of the trader's hands.

TABB: It also depends on what you are trying to trade. Crossing systems tend to do much better with small-cap and small mid-cap stocks. This is because small and mid-cap stocks do not trade that frequently, and traders usually do not worry as much about VWAP. The other question is how much of that liquidity is out there in any given name at any given time?

The other issue is the business model. Some of the crossing networks are actually more expensive than using algorithms. If I am going to go buy a gazillion shares of Microsoft, I might as well just pay the minimum for it and trade it in an algorithm all day. It is cheaper and less risky. If it is a small-cap stock and I am trying to trade 50% or a 100% of its average daily volume? This is a very different type of animal. This brings us back again to the silver bullet. I do not believe that there is a silver bullet.

UNIDENTIFIED SPEAKER: Just a quick comment. On the buy-side you are given a whole new set of tools. These tools can now take an input alpha and, based on that information, decide how to trade it, as opposed to simply not knowing the objective and how to trade in the market. Some clients will want to do alpha all day, or perhaps have some other goal on strategy. Others recognize high alpha and they want to get right in there.

HARTS: Yes, sir.

UNIDENTIFIED SPEAKER: I do not think that anyone has mentioned how Reg NMS will play out in all of this. It seems to have gone by the wayside. The other thing is, I am sure that all of you have estimated the percentage of market share that you hope to attain, and it probably adds up to more than a hundred. Relating that back to Reg NMS, what do you think the NYSE and NASDAQ will either gain or lose in market share under it? I have heard estimates all over the lot including gains of substantial amounts, and losses of substantial amounts. What do you think?

HARTS: I asked that question at last year's conference. I did not get a great answer. I still do not think that the industry has a great answer. As you pointed out, the estimates are widely different.

BERKELEY: At Pipeline we will obviously comply with Reg NMS. We believe that if the friction costs of trading were lower, the amount of trading would be a lot higher. Our portfolio manager from Maine implied that. I do not think that there is any problem with new markets claiming to have more than 100% of the existing market. Some of these markets can be 50% or 100% bigger than they are today if you take some of the excruciatingly painful costs of front running and market impact out of the picture.

What I am saying is that you can grow the pie. As for Reg NMS, we built Pipeline to try to solve the same problems that NMS is trying to solve. But we used a free market approach rather than a regulatory approach. We did not get out fast enough, and the regulatory response developed its own political momentum. It is well intentioned. Reg NMS will undoubtedly have some unintended consequences that none of us can foresee right now.

HARTS: Does anyone want to take a stab in the dark as to what Reg NMS will mean for competition between markets?

TABB: We will see more volume flow to the regional exchanges. However, in the longer term, liquidity wants to centralize, so most of these regional exchanges will, therefore, either consolidate or become immaterial. Eventually, in the U.S., we will see only three or four markets succeed. The costs are too low and the pressures too high for there to be two or three exchanges splitting 75% of the market share, while seven or eight exchanges split 15% and dark pools capture the other 10%.

HARTS: The first question you have to ask is, when might Reg NMS take effect? Then you can say what the effects will be.

TABB: If it will ever go. There are so many ifs here, but the way things are set up it basically incents folks to put liquidity in the regional exchanges. The routing engines generally go from the fastest to the slowest markets (given equal pricing). If the limit orders go out to the regionals and the regionals tend to be faster than the central core, they will get matched first. Then there will be less liquidity in the center. Whether the NYSE goes down to 60%, or 50%, or 40% depends upon whether the regional infrastructure gets up to speed, how fast they are, and the rebates that they will offer.[10]

There are some that are trading at a mil – net a mil – which is pretty damn cheap. There are a whole bunch of different ifs. But that is the way the regs are written. You are starting to see the brokers investing in the regionals. The question will be, what happens when some of this stuff gets turned on? Will it work, and will the routing engines go at the right speed? That is for the regional guys to do.

BERKELEY: I predict that the next big issue will be payment for order flow and rebates. It is a classic principal-agent problem. As that money gets larger and larger, somebody in the corporate governance world, or somewhere, will get on to it.

---

[10] As of October 2007, the New York Stock Exchange matched some 40% percent of the volume of all NYSE-listed trades, according to industry analyst Richard Repetto and published statistics.

HARTS: Yes?

STEPHEN SAX (Floor Broker Network) [From the Floor]: We are members of the New York Stock Exchange as floor brokers. The crossing networks represented here on the panel are a relatively new concept. I understand that you have a lot of smart institutional participants. On the floor of the New York Stock Exchange, block trades are executed every day until 4:00 p.m. All that time and every minute in the day, the exchange is available to do blocks. On these crossing networks it seems you get an execution. It stays in the system. My question is, at a certain period of time, is getting a big block done maybe just about an ease of transaction? If it fits in the system, couldn't somebody get a better price, before the transaction actually transacts? Is it really the right price? Or, is it just because it is easy to do a cross on a large size? But once again, is the price right?

HARTS: It never hurts to end with a question, and we are out of time. Thanks, everybody.

Chapter 6
The Countervailing Power of the Buy-Side

**Michael Murphy, George Bodine, Paul Davis, Mark Forziati,
Tim Mahoney, and Mony Rueven**

MICHAEL MURPHY: The title of the panel is "The Countervailing Power of the Buy-Side." Earlier, I had asked six people to define the word countervailing before I was eventually able to figure it out.

Now that I understand it, I am reminded of Bob Dylan's song, "The Times They Are A-Changing." Well, that is happening today. Regulations have changed the markets. Commission rates are heading lower, driven by a more transparent marketplace and technological innovations by both brokers and investment managers. The innovations include electronic systems like Instinet and POSIT, as well as dark pools of liquidity, while brokers have moved into the program trading game to recoup some of the dollars subsequently lost. At the same time, brokers and investment banks have moved aggressively into the very profitable derivative marketplace.

This compression on rates and the shift of power from the sell-side to the buy-side, are probably largely driven by technology and the better application of this technology. About 5 or 6 years ago we were trying to implement technological changes at the New York Stock Exchange and in other places. A lot of people were putting up their hands and asking us to wait. I said at the time that there is more technology out there now than we know what to do with it. The problem is that there are not enough people who know how to use it.

In 4, 5, 6 or 7 years time, when some of the people out of school – well, they are here now – come to work on Wall Street, we will see more changes. They know how to operate the technology. They grew up with it. I have three teenage daughters in college. I used to say it is kind of like how I started taking lessons in French when I was 40. My kids had started lessons at six! I can find the sign for the bathroom, or maybe order a bottle of wine in France, whereas this comes naturally to my kids. It is no big deal.

Similarly, unlike many people of my generation, my kids think a lot about sophisticated technology and know how to apply it. Technology has driven a lot of changes – and there will be a lot more because of the new professionals entering the trading business. These are all the young people who grew up in a technologically-advanced society, in the era of online banking and brokerage. These same people are applying their extraordinary technological skills in the world of electronic and algorithmic trading. I applaud them. That is a great development for the industry.

R.A. Schwartz et al. (eds.), *Competition in a Consolidating Environment*,
doi: 10.1007/978-0-387-75943-2_6, © Springer Science+Business Media, LLC 2008

I do a lot of public speaking. I have been involved in many market structure issues and panels. Hopefully, there will be plenty of thoughtful questions raised on this panel. I guarantee that there will be thoughtful answers. On this distinguished panel are Paul Davis, TIAA-CREF; George Bodine, who runs trading at General Motors; Mark Forziati who runs trading at Tudor Investment Corporation, one of the large hedge funds. There is also Tim Mahoney, who heads Merrill Lynch Asset Management. Finally, there is Mony Rueven who runs trading at D.E. Shaw, also one of the largest hedge funds.

We are especially glad to have Mark and Mony here because in the conference world there has been a lack of views expressed by the hedge funds. People talk about how these guys are doing their businesses, but we generally hear it indirectly.

Everybody here runs their business a bit differently. I will start with you, George. What is the most important thing that you risk losing today? Clearly there is a shift of power to the buy-side, and a shift of service away from the brokerage communities, the traditional brokers. What do you risk losing in this environment?

GEORGE BODINE: In a way, the brokers are providing a much more customized service today. We think of the traditional broker as helping us on the research side and the single stock side. Brokers were extremely valuable providing that research. Then along came Reg FD.[1] With that, the timeliness of the research – and maybe the special client arrangement that you would get that first call – was neutralized.

Under Reg FD, the importance that the brokers had given to individual accounts was now spread out, so that everyone was treated evenly. Also, a lot of the research opinions that the brokers used to release intraday to certain clients were instead released either before the opening, or after the closing, so that everyone had a chance to react. Before Reg FD, if I was an important client of, say, Goldman Sachs, I might get the first call telling me that their top analyst was going to recommend or downgrade some company. That would give me an advantage over other investors. Today, under Reg FD, Goldman has to release the same information to all investors equally.

Another area that has changed in market structure, from the buy-side to the sell-side, are the IPO allocations. These allocations were always lucrative and profitable for the buy-side. Brokers would allocate the largest proportion of shares in an IPO to their most profitable buy-side clients. In the process, a dialogue took place between the sales traders on the sell-side and his counterparts on the buy-side. The sales trader who was influential internally at his firm would lobby for his buy-side clients to get the most shares of stock. That scenario has changed with electronic trading and the reduction in the size of the typical commission payment.

---

[1] Regulation Fair Disclosure, or Reg FD, was enacted by the U.S. Securities and Exchange Commission in 2006. The regulation requires all publicly-traded companies to disclose material information to all investors at the same time. The goal is to eliminate selective disclosure of this information to certain groups of investors, usually institutions, who had the advantage of receiving potentially market-moving information before other investors. See, www.sec.gov/rules/final/33–7881.htm.

The role of the sales trader has changed in the process and, consequently, your influence as a buy-side customer has been undercut. Your commission payments have less currency now even if you are still trading the same number of shares. For example, if you are paying 2 cents a share today, compared with a nickel a share in the past, that is 40% of what you used to pay. Of course, if all participants are equally affected by these changes, then this is not the same issue. However, I don't think the impact of this change in the IPO allocation structure is evenly distributed.

Commission compression is a significant change. If you are paying five cents a share, you are getting a certain amount of value for that nickel. Now, if you are paying 2 cents, a penny and a half, or one cent a share, something has to give. We are losing a lot of the customization and the special handling that had been available to us all along. On the other hand, we are getting, more do-it-yourself services from brokers like, for instance, the Goldman Sachs REDIPlus products. With these services, you are able to customize your strategies with algorithms and do a lot of the work, such as pre-trade analysis. In the past, you would depend more on a human trader to do this for you. Today, it has really become a self-service model for the buy-side. This is probably more indicative of the world we live in. Think about it. If you go to book an airline ticket you are doing the reservation yourself. You are checking in at the airline kiosk yourself. If you go to Home Depot, you can scan the products you buy and complete the checkout yourself. Well, our market is not any different. We have the order. We are directing it and driving it, and we are timing it ourselves. We have been provided the tools to do this.

MURPHY: Mark?

MARK FORZIATI: Before I start, I just want to say that my comments do not reflect Tudor Investments. These are my own personal views. And sometimes they are so radical I do not think any of you will have similar views. As George says, with commissions on a downward spiral for the past few years, our needs are certainly different. Commissions really do not come into play in our case. We are performance-driven to the point where we get a management fee as well as performance fee. If we perform well, we will get compensated. Consequently, we are looking for research. We are looking for service.

As Wall Street wrestles with decimalization, Reg NMS, and more automation, you are seeing a slippage in the traditional service we have been accustomed to over the past 15 years. It is a problem because we see more and more fragmentation within the marketplace. There are now 15 different alternative trading systems/ECNs out there. Fifteen! On a daily basis, we are trying to access the various pools of liquidity. We are not just looking for an average of 200 shares per trade. We are not just looking for 500 shares. We are actually looking for hundreds of thousands of shares to complete our large blocks, and yet we are executing all these smaller individual trades to accomplish this. It is hard to access liquidity when you have these so-called dark pools of liquidity fragmented across the market. And as George Bodine says, with technology so pervasive today in our society, at times Wall Street seems to (or at least some firms seem to) – fight it as opposed to embrace it.

We can talk about the New York Stock Exchange and its hybrid system. But from my perspective, it is becoming increasingly difficult to get good service in the traditional fashion. This includes finding pools of liquidity without having to ask brokers to commit capital. Transparency is another big, big factor. In the old days, in certain situations, you would know who traded a block of stock and was active in the name. Nowadays, this same transparency is gone. With the elimination of Rule 390, NYSE member firms can now also trade large listed blocks away from the exchange in different names on the Third Market – on NASDAQ – and do not have to advertise them. Before the elimination of the rule, these same names were always traded on the floor of the NYSE where it was possible to find out what firms were trading the stock and other important information. For instance, I could find out, or get a sense of whether or not I could buy some stock, or could I sell some stock? That kind of transparency is no longer there.

MURPHY: Tim?

TIM MAHONEY: I am not nearly as funny as Mark, but Ill try. When I think about this panel I think about Thomas Friedman's book, "*The World is Flat*,"[2] and I reflect on what we spoke about that this morning. Here are a couple of things. Clearly, he is writing about our type of industry. He said the world is flat. And so is our industry. The responsibilities of the buy-side and the sell-side have been flattened, so to speak, so that the differences that had separated them have blurred significantly. We are now empowered and accountable for a lot of the traditional goods and services that the sell-side has provided to us.

Friedman tells the story of a woman who lived in Boston and then moved to San Francisco. Coming back to Boston for the weekend, her friend asked, "Hey, how do you like San Francisco? She replied, 'It is great, except I miss the ocean.'" And that is how we view the world too. We miss the fact that the Pacific Ocean is actually an ocean. We just do not realize this even though it is right there in front of our eyes. I mean, the world has fundamentally changed over the years. If you take fragmented pools of liquidity and interlink them, you essentially have a network. That is what we have now. We are living in a networked world. As it has been flattened out, we now have the ability to execute lots of orders in lots of different places. My tickets have ten or 15 different destinations for the same order. In the past you could go to one destination and complete a trade; now you must go to multiple places. The Pacific and the Atlantic are both oceans, but they are still different. By the same token, executing 1 million shares in one trade is different than executing 1 million shares in 1,000 separate trades, even though, in both cases, you execute the same number of shares.

Over the last couple of years, our transaction costs have come down each and every year. So I am not sure if there is an inefficient market in place today. I do think, however, that it is a more difficult market. It is far more complex. And that is okay. Quite frankly, the more complex it gets, the more valuable our skills become as traders.

---

[2] *The World Is Flat: A Brief History of the Twenty-first Century*, Thomas L. Friedman, Farrar, Straus and Giroux, 2005.

And the more valuable to me traditional skills are. Now buy-side traders are really trading. We now have the responsibility for the actual decisions that we make. We can execute orders on our own. We can be held accountable. So I cannot imagine a better time to be in this job. The only other thing better is being Mike Murphy!

FORZIATI: You are saying that you have the ability to monitor your transaction costs, and they are going down? Transaction costs in terms of market impact as well?

MAHONEY: Yes.

FORZIATI: Then you must be using alternative trading systems, not the traditional platforms?

MAHONEY: Yes. Right now we use everything. I would say that there is a continuum of services that you can use – from the simplest DMA product right up to using a capital markets desk, which is the interface between investment banking and the equity trading desk, as well as a variety of ATSs, including Pipeline and ITG's DarkServer. At the end of the day, you capture the data. You know what your impact cost is. You know what your commission costs are. You know what your slippage and performance is. All that matters is how good your performance is at the end of the day. You now have the ability to quantify exactly what it is you do and how much slippage is related to what you do. It is no longer, "Gee, I gave a trade to Broker X and the result was bad. He must not be any good." Now, it is about having the ability to do a variety of different things with your trade. Broker X is just one of the possible choices I have in my trading decision. I am responsible for the choice.

MURPHY: Mony, I am glad that you are here. Tell us a little bit about what you are doing

MONY RUEVEN: These views are my own personal opinions and not those of D. E. Shaw. We are in an interesting, evolutionary period. It is a period where one needs to think about the role of a broker. In the future, will broker-dealers operate more as dealers than brokers?

MURPHY: What do you think?

RUEVEN: Will we really need brokers in the future? Will the broker be just a destination point? Who are we on the buy-side? We are liquidity seekers. We seek liquidity all the time. We are just looking for liquidity. The days when brokers find the other side of a trade are numbered. Where are we going to go to find the liquidity? Liquidity is in a destination. Since we are pretty much looking for liquidity all the time, I am really worried about there being 15 different ECNs, ATSs and the like. The technology required to be in every one of them, and actually manage a book in every one of them, is very complex. It is a huge undertaking. You cannot just slice and dice and say, "Okay, I am going to go out and find something."

I believe that the first VWAP trading system was introduced on Wall Street in the early 1990s In fact, I think we are now too hung up on VWAP – Volume Weighted Average Price – in this marketplace. Once a standard becomes a measurement, and a measurement becomes a standard, it is no longer any good. To get the trade done as cheaply as possible – sometimes slicing it, and using VWAP and all this stuff – is now costing you more money. You must think about how you capture Alpha.

MURPHY: Paul? Do you want to add something here?

PAUL DAVIS: I agreed more with Tim than with Mark. The opportunities for traders today are superb. Brokers are responding quite well to the changes that are happening in our industry. Many brokers, I won't say all, but many are, as George Sofianos said, giving us a full spectrum of execution services. If a trader knows how to really use the services that the broker supplies, the trader can do an excellent job. I see that our traders are looking to brokers more for capital commitments now than they used to.[3] A number of brokers are stepping up. We find oftentimes that the capital commitment is consistent with what the portfolio manager wants. The PM is willing to pay a price to get the execution in place. Other times we slice and dice. There are a lot of good tools on the trader's desk now.

Traders also sometimes have a lot more discretion in how to work the orders. On other occasions, the decision is made for them by the portfolio manager. But we can work our way through the decision-making process, getting a sense of what is happening. In many respects, these are some of the better times in my years in the trading business.

MURPHY: Questions from the audience.

MARC GRESACK (MatchPoint Trading) [From the Floor]: George, this is a follow-up to Reg FD. Would you, or the panel, comment on the issues of liquidity and price discovery in the after-hours market? As an investor, I find that in most of the stocks that I own, where the reports are made after the close, price discovery is at best lumpy, and it continues that way until the next day when the market actually opens. Can you comment on that and its impact on performance?

BODINE: If the event occurs between, say, 4:00 p.m. and 5:00 p.m., it is lumpy, sure, but it seems that the market is fairly efficient and fairly well organized. There are enough market participants to create liquidity. If the event comes sometime after 5:00 p.m., or at 6:00 p.m., or 7:00 p.m., it really creates a bigger impact, because there are not as many participants and not as much liquidity. It is like this with a Microsoft earnings announcement at these later hours. The impact will be much bigger, and has a kind of domino effect if you are trading futures, or the S&P 500 and the Nasdaq 100, in which Microsoft is a big component.

Within an hour or so of the close, most people are still there. They are reacting to the market, and you can get some good information. Hopefully, supply and demand will find their equilibrium. After that, it really tends to be a crapshoot. You take your best guess. You may be totally right on the analysis and the numbers that

---

[3] Trading professionals noted a renewed interest in capital commitment during this period, following an earlier decline that coincided with the introduction of penny trading increments in 2001 on the NYSE and Nasdaq. The move to penny trading is cited for the sharp reduction in the average size of equity trades in the institutional markets, which curbed capital committed in block trading. Greenwich Associates estimated that 14% of all institutional volume in 2005 required a capital commitment, declining to 12% in 2006. Anecdotal evidence, however, suggested that several bulge bracket firms were becoming more aggressive in committing capital. This was partly a result of competition from electronic trading and dark pools of liquidity, as well as demand from the buy-side.

you wanted, but you are never trading on the numbers. You are trading on company expectation about their earnings. You are also trading on Street perception, which may be at odds with this expectation. The company may expect earnings of 20 cents a share, for example, whereas the bulk of investors could think that 25 cents is a more accurate number. These expectations and perceptions may be fuelled by rumors on the Street about earnings; or by an analyst on CNBC. That is always the challenging part.

One of the difficulties that I see with electronic trading (and I do a lot of it), is that you do not always get that important piece of information that will give you a hint of what to expect. You have this utility that lets you distribute an order, but it does not come back and say, "Wait a minute, you should slow up!" You are going too fast with your order! I miss the human contact, the interaction and flow of information that the brokers could provide.

MURPHY: Yes, Isabelle.

ISABELLE CLARY (Financial News) [From the Floor]: Now that you can access liquidity anywhere, is there any merit left to the notion that liquidity begets liquidity?

FORZIATI: Yes, I would agree that liquidity begets liquidity. There are times when you are looking for liquidity and, as Paul Davis said, you may call a broker and ask the broker to commit capital. They are very generous with the capital they commit to large institutions. They will typically find the other side in a large-cap listed name in a transaction that is transparent and, consequently, that promotes liquidity. The broker will advertise the block of listed stock say, 100,000 shares, in a liquid stock. This will typically prompt other traders on algorithmic systems, or on dark pools, working individual trades of 200–300 shares, to get off their hands to sell the stock. Once these traders see Merrill Lynch advertise the block, they will go, "Wow, let's call Merrill." Next thing you know, they have sold the block of stock to Merrill. That helps Merrill get out of its position, after committing capital and selling me the block, and the trade takes place between Merrill and the seller of the stock on the other side. Clearly, this creates more liquidity in the market.

Transparency depends on market conditions. In this example, there is transparency, which is good for liquidity, and liquidity does beget liquidity. But, as I mentioned earlier, as far as I am concerned, there has actually been a decrease in market transparency because of changes in market structure.

Once again, in these so-called dark pools of liquidity, everyone is sort of operating in a nocturnal environment. Then all of a sudden, a light goes on and everyone says, Okay, I need to trade.

UNIDENTIFIED SPEAKER: I have a caveat. Assume that someone has an algorithm on one side, and a VWAP model that I do not have. Suppose I am trading on last nights close. I may find the other side, but I have not done anything about it, even though this person has the size I want to trade. So, he is tied into this VWAP model and, if I have 800,000 shares to trade; maybe I get 25,000 done at a clip. Each time. I am ready and willing to trade, I am on the other side, and there is an equal contra-side. But their strategy is different, so we just do not get the trade done.

RUEVEN: I do not think that there is an application out there that actually ties both of the algos and blocks together. That would probably be the next killer application, something that ties them together, so that you can actually be electronic everywhere, and also do a block at the same time. You could have two different market participants who actually want to do the same thing; both, say, want to get down 1,000 shares of the stock. Somebody wants to do it right now, and they are willing to do it at the very best price.

MURPHY: Yes?

DOUG ATKIN (Majestic Research) [From the Floor]: I have two questions. First, how are you measuring the effectiveness of the brokers in terms of measuring trading costs? Second, with everything that is going on with the famous Fidelity/Lehman Brothers announcement,[4] what are your organizations doing regarding both soft dollars and handling the vote.[5] Do you see changes in how you are doling out commissions to Wall Street?

MURPHY: Someone else want to talk?

MAHONEY: As for measuring costs, the implementation shortfall[6] has always been a good way to look at it. I do not know if Mark Wright is still around, but the ITG product does a nice job in this area. It tells you what your true costs are from the time you get the order to the time it is executed. You can talk about whether it is good or bad, (which is more subjective), but certainly it is the slippage in your performance that you should look at.

If it is soft dollars, we think a lot about that, but we also remember that the numbers are very interesting. A penny a share represents about 4 basis points in performance, all other things being equal. For a portfolio manager to go from the 50th percentile to the top quartile in the Lipper Large-Cap Value Funds Index we calculated that the PM needs to improve his performance by 200 basis points, based on data in the same period which we gathered. However, if you are concentrating on the soft-dollar component, or the explicit commission rate, keep in mind that if you are paying 4 cents a share, you can only pick up about 16 basis points by eliminating explicit commissions. So, improving performance in this scenario is a complicated dynamic. Our clients have told us that it is their money, and they want us to maximize the value to them. That is what we try to do.

---

[4] In late 2005, Fidelity and Lehman Brothers entered into a research unbundling relationship. According to reports, Fidelity agreed to pay Lehman $7 million in actual cash for research while Lehman, in turn, would charge Fidelity an unbundled commission rate of 2 cents to 2.5 cents for execution, according to industry reports. The industry average for "blended commissions" was estimated at 3.6 cents.

[5] Buy-side firms will allocate commission dollars to their executing brokers in proportion to the preferences, or votes cast by certain members of these buy-side firms for research services in soft-dollar arrangements.

[6] Implementation shortfall, or slippage, measures the difference between the decision price (such as the close price of a stock) and the final, all-inclusive execution price.

ANTHONY FORTUNATO (Instinet, LLC)[7] [From the Floor]: You are talking about blocks, and the frustrations today in block trading. I do not know anybody who sets out in the morning and says, my price target to own or sell this stock is VWAP. But for some reason these blocks tend to trade that way.

RUEVEN: What I see out there is a big slicing engine. Most of the engines are using similar technology for slicing orders. They all follow the same trend and trade the same way. The only difference is the frequency of the slice. Basically, if you look at other brokers – which include all the DMA products – they all do the VWAP. The only thing that has changed over the years is the frequency, the time between one slice and the next slice. From a slippage point of view, I like its limitations. Once you get it, that is where you start to measure.

MURPHY: How many of these people do you think actually meet or beat VWAP with these algorithms?

RUEVEN: Most of them meet VWAP. Very few beat it.

SPEAKER: I am going to argue most of them slip.

MURPHY: Whether its 25 mils or 50 mils?

RUEVEN: It is got to be…

MURPHY: And so who do you think is picking up the 25 or 50?

FORZIATI: No, that is the part of the slippage from, perhaps, the inefficiency of the marketplace. There are 15 different systems out there. If the market was truly efficient, we would have just one exchange or one venue to trade securities, and have one sort of price discovery system that would not be fragmenting the market. Consequently, you will have that slippage.

Of course, it is a kind of zero sum game. If someone is beating the VWAP, someone is losing against the VWAP. Something like VWAP works pretty well in a very low volatility environment. So with the VIX[8] at historic lows, you can afford to be patient. But if volatility were to pick up again, you would see people abandoning those strategies on a more wholesale basis.

MURPHY: At the end of quarter, at the end of the year, if you have great performance, does your client really care about how much commissions you charge? Or if you meet the VWAP? Do they care if you are soft-dollaring four cents a share of your commissions?

DAVIS: They care about everything. Clients are now much more sophisticated. Our boards want to know not only what our performance is, but how we got there. What process the portfolio manager uses. What process we use. How do we allocate trades? How do we measure trades? What is the trend in measuring them? What are our commissions? How do we know the right commission? How do we select brokers?

[7] At the time of the conference, Mr. Fortunato was Director of U.S. Equity Sales and Trading at Nomura Securities International.

[8] VIX, for the Chicago Board Options Exchange Volatility Index, measure the implied volatility of S&P 500 index options.

Technology has allowed traders to get further into the process. They have become more sophisticated. But I do believe, as Michael said, that clients will give you money based on how good your performance is. That is the final determinate. But they want to have access to all the information that comes into that final number.

BODINE: I wear two hats for General Motors Asset Management. We are a pension manager that hires outside managers as well as being large enough to have our own internal trading desk. I review the outside manager's traders and handle my own as well. Probably 80% of our assets are managed externally. So I am the customer of these outside managers. We manage about 20% of the money internally, so my trades are all scrutinized by my superiors.

When I have my hat on to visit the outside managers, I really challenge them as to why they made decisions that they did. Not to be duplicitous when they review mine, we have to be pretty regimented as to how we handle that.

We did eliminate our third-party soft dollars. We paid hard dollars for those because I could not just ask, why are you doing all this soft-dollar business, couldn't you be using your money more wisely? It is a slippery slope because it is very difficult to find a true measurement of performance. Try looking at a trade order measurement system two or three months after the fact. It is extremely difficult to get a true picture of what happened.

We would like nothing more than a clear picture, but unfortunately there is so much inconsistency. In one period, one broker and one trader could look terrible in the measurements, but in the next period the same broker at the same firm could do an excellent job.

You do not have that ability to say, wait a minute, you did a poor job using these brokers. We try to be as diligent as we can looking at who we use and the money that we pay. We use an implementation shortfall as our primary measurement. But what we show our board is the overall cost of trading. With anything other than that, we always have caveats. As soon as you drill down to see what that one broker is doing, or what one trader is doing, the data get very, very noisy. But at the aggregate level, we are comfortable with the numbers we see. We are happy to say that trading costs have come down over the last half a dozen years or so because there is more competition. There is more electronic trading and more venues to trade.

MURPHY: Do you guys run pension money also?

RUEVEN: I cannot talk about that. However, I will say that the market is moving into more real-time transaction cost measurement, which will change the way we all trade. As we get real-time feedback, one will be able to change tactics, and ones approach to trading intra-day.

I agree with Paul. We are living in a very exciting time. Actually, right now is a great time to be in the industry because there are so many changes. Nobody can really predict what the future will hold. Look at the market, look at the exchanges, and at all the ATSs and ECNs. You know there will be at least a huge evolution similar to the early introduction of ECNs. It started, say, with two ECNs, and now you have a lot of ATSs. They will come together. The technology will become better and faster. It will be a lot of fun.

FORZIATI: I guess the best measurement of trade analysis is the fact that my boss keeps a baseball bat in his desk! But seriously, as a hedge fund, we cannot use VWAP or any different type of algorithmic system, particularly if we are short. VWAP does not apply in a lot of hedge fund trading because of the nature of our positions. We have to be aggressive in closing out a position. For example, if you were short Google, and it suddenly is added to the S&P 500,[9] it is a matter of getting the trade done as quickly as possible with the minimum amount of market impact.

We are very good at monitoring the brokers. My boss is very good at analyzing the trades. We all do that. But at some point, we probably will have to have some formal monitoring system. That is because the SEC is regulating hedge funds, and we will probably have to get into compliance with them sometime soon.

MAHONEY: Mike, the added benefit of Transaction Cost Analysis is that if you give the trade to your traders, they can reduce their transaction costs. From our perspective, we let our guys look at the TCA every day. And they have literally gotten better at what they do because it is as if they have a P&L. If you are in a hedge fund, you have a P&L to a great extent.

For a long time on the buy-side, we had the luxury of saying that we really were good at what we do; but that we cannot be measured on how we do our job. Now you have this product and it is able to say, "Hey, this is what your costs were." Of course, interpreting those costs is tricky. I will tell you that you cannot take any econometric model – whether it is the PAEG/L[10] or ACE[11] – and make it an absolute, but you know what your trend is all the same. You know what the cost is. If you are looking at your trades every day, you will get better at it. You will be able to say, "Gee, that cost me 70 basis points." Maybe if I had done something different I could have gotten that cost down. The next time we do the trade you may take a different approach to it. Focusing on little pieces of it is part of the process of total investment performance.

This is a very competitive business – at every level. Everything you can do to save a couple of basis points here and there adds to the final performance numbers for the overall investors.

MURPHY: Got a question there?

UNIDENTIFIED SPEAKER [From the Floor]: Based on what you guys have seen thus far of the NYSE hybrid market, how satisfied are you with it and how likely are you to use it?

FORZIATI: You do not have a gun on you, do you, Peter? Just kidding. We just came back from the NYSE. I believe George was there, and Michael, you were there as well? We are also just back from a conference in Washington. The Exchange would admit that it is a work in progress, and that it will be making

---

[9] Google was added to the S&P 500 prior to the conference.

[10] Plexus Average Execution Gain/Loss, a benchmark of ITG.

[11] Agency Cost Estimator from ITG that provides pre-trade cost analysis "'as well as the ability to handicap trades for relative and absolute trade difficulty,'" according to ITG.

adjustments to hybrid. I will certainly try it and see how it plays out. But the Exchange will be the first to admit that we are entering this new world. If they have to tweak it going forward, they will do so. Think about the topic of this panel – "The Countervailing Power of the Buy-Side." Well, if the buy-side is not satisfied, that certainly will put pressure on the Exchange, and on other venues. These, in turn, will make changes in response to the buy-side's demands.

MAHONEY: The key to success for the hybrid is how well it handles the small mid-cap stocks. I do not think you will find anybody who disagrees that large stocks will trade mostly electronically. However, with a hybrid, will it be mostly price discovery in small to mid-cap stocks? Does the specialist now have the opportunity, unencumbered by trading large-caps like GE, to make better, more robust markets in the mid-cap stocks to bring buyers and sellers together in the traditional sense? We will only know over time. But that will give the specialists an opportunity to make better markets in small to mid-cap stocks. We all recognize that there are certainly parts of the marketplace that need more human touch and intervention by traders than others.

BOB WOOD (University of Memphis) [From the Floor]: A question about VWAP trading. My understanding is that the basic idea is that we will take an order that we might trade as a block, but instead split it up and parse it out through the day based on U-shaped volume.[12] We will put it up as a limit order for, let us say, five minutes. If it does not work, we flip it to a marketable limit order. Then we will put up the limit order. We can get smarter doing that by looking at the futures/spot basis in real time, to pick up prices switching from mean-reverting to trending, to improve our strategy. Could anybody comment on that?

RUEVEN: On a theoretical basis, you are absolutely correct. But the time intervals are getting shorter. That is the issue. Participants do not have the patience of six minutes to sit on the bid and then wait and go to the midpoint, and eventually go to the offer. The time frames are shrinking fast, so you have to move fast. If you look at the trend in the marketplace, you will find that as the day progresses you will see more and more market orders and less limit orders.

You probably can do a great job trading VWAP in the top 100 liquid names. You can slice it all in one day. But as you move away from the top liquid names, it becomes harder and harder to do. The liquidity becomes scarcer. Of course, if you are about 25% of the ADV,[13] you, in effect, set the daily VWAP.

The systems are pretty much trying to answer the same question all the time: What is the next volume slice going to be, and are we going to do it? I see trading systems taking more risk in their design, and they are not just depending on algorithms. They are trying to not only predict volume, but also to predict price. The algorithm becomes a bit more risky.

---

[12] This means volume that is heaviest in early and late trading day; lighter during the middle of the trading day.

[13] Average Daily Volume.

MAHONEY: The VWAP was a first-generation algorithm. Five years ago that was the first thing you had to help you increase productivity, to handle orders that you had no view about. Back then, volatility had collapsed, so there was less risk involved. The markets were not as volatile and, in a less volatile market similar to this period, VWAP is a fine strategy. Now there are a hundred different strategies. Some are better than others. The challenge (Larry Tabb has written a lot about this) is to determine which algorithm works. When do you use which one, and under what circumstance?

We have more tools now than ever before to get to the same result. You have to figure out which one of those tools will work for you. What works depends on whether it is a block trade, or, whether a dark server or an AES[14] is being used. In certain circumstances, maybe VWAP is appropriate. You will know at the end of the day whether or not it has worked. It all feeds back into the ultimate end performance for your client.

MURPHY: Has the shift in the how broker-dealers are employing their capital impacted your business? As you know, brokers have moved capital from their equity desks into prop trading, so it seems that there is less capital available on the dealer side. Are broker-dealers committing capital nowadays?

MAHONEY: Capital is really interesting. Brokers who commit capital would hope (like Mike Murphy in his days on the buy-side) that you do more business with them. That becomes less likely now that we have so many choices, and there are so many alternative sources of liquidity.

The pricing of capital is changing dramatically. Brokers have come to the conclusion that there must be a fairer price because it is unlikely that they will get more flow next time just because they were nice guys this time around. It has become a far more dynamic situation where you still use capital and try to be more thoughtful about when you use capital.

Last year there were a couple of really large trades. That becomes interesting when you use capital, maybe even not just in block trading, but in truly capital market arrangements. You have guys who sit on both sides of the Chinese Wall at the capital markets desks at investment banks who interface with the buy-side, as well as companies that want to become public. If you are from the buy-side and you call the capital markets desk, they are not permitted to tell the equity trading desk. In any event, deals become fascinating in this environment.

BODINE: We do a lot of program trades and package trades on the domestic trades. We probably beat VWAP one out of five times domestically. But if I am trading in the Far East, in Japan or in Europe, I beat VWAP more often.

MURPHY: Paul?

DAVIS: First, I am thinking about the tone and emotions of you guys over the past five or so years. My sense is that you are much more accepting of the current situation. That you are more agnostic about it. I hear you saying that trading costs

---

[14] Advanced Execution Service (AES) is the algorithmic trading services of Credit Suisse.

have come down as you have measured them. That could be consistent with your having less to gripe about. My other observation, which gets back to the title of the conference ("Competition in a Consolidating Environment" is close to my heart), is the following. I have heard a lot of discussion about competition. I do not know if it is just my perception, but I do not hear as much discussion about consolidation. Last year at this time, there was a lot of discussion in Europe about consolidation in relation to three exchanges possibly becoming two. There was also a lot happening here in the U.S. because of NYSE and Archipelago, and NASDAQ and Instinet.

My question is, when all is said and done, would you guys be happier, and feel that you could do your job more effectively, if we were operating in a more consolidated environment? I am asking this because I hear a lot of talk about fragmentation, multiple vendors, and multiple ATSs.

FORZIATI: It depends on the kind of a consolidated market. If it is an order-driven electronic market, and that is all that is out there, I would not be a happy camper. We need choice. We need competition to keep the brokers on their toes, to keep the exchanges on their toes. There has to be different venues for different types of orders.

MURPHY: I will put all the good choice words together - How about a consolidated hybrid?

DAVIS: Well, yes, when we figure out what that is, it might be wonderful. But we do not know what that is yet.

FORZIATI: I have to disagree with Paul. First of all, I am not complacent. Second, it is interesting that Mony and I seem to be on the same page (being at hedge funds) versus Tim and Paul who work at traditional money management firms. I do not know where George stands on this issue. But you talk about consolidation. I would say that if you had one central marketplace, there will still be competition. There are brokers. There are retailers. The wholesalers have massive amounts of order flow. Everyone in this room, I am sure, may have an account at E*Trade, Ameritrade, wherever. Those orders are getting internalized. They are not seeing the New York Stock Exchange or NASDAQ. They are not getting into the marketplace.

George talks about VWAP being done overseas, and that he gets better results there. I trade electronically overseas. Sometimes I do not even look at a screen. I just ask the broker what is the quote. He gives me the depth of the market, and I say okay, take it. At least in the Asian market, nothing will trade that will prevent me from getting that liquidity. It is all there.

Accordingly, the broker can say, "Gee, I know that there are a million shares for sale, so I will sell you 2 million shares." You can't do that on the New York Stock Exchange. I am not faulting the NYSE. I am faulting the participants. Let me say consolidation. Again, a radical idea. Within 5–10 years we will have a lot fewer brokerage firms.

The unbundling by Fidelity and Lehman Brothers was mentioned earlier. I have analysts who are constantly approaching us as a consequence of Reg FD. I am like, who are these people and where did they come from? Perhaps they worked at

Lehman Brothers, and started their own little boutique research firm. We have to pay them. I do not know how well they trade. So what do you do in these types of situation? You go to an ECN, unbundle the commission, and you say "Okay, at the end of the month, we will send them a check for the research provided."

Just think of how many brokerage firms do not have investment banking relationships. Morgan Stanley can bring you a Google IPO. A lot of firms do not have investment banking. They will provide you pure vanilla research. Do you really need to trade with them? No, you do not. You can trade electronically and then have the commissions sent. It is happening now. In England, the FSA, is light years ahead of the SEC in the unbundling process.[15] You are seeing larger firms approaching these mid-size firms and saying "Eliminate your trading desks and just provide the research."[16]

RUEVEN: The changes in the marketplace will begin with people. We are starting to see a new breed of traders who use computer keyboards instead of the telephone to communicate. They IM all day long and are not building relationships. That is why the focus is on speed of execution and not about the art of trading. That will force changes in the exchanges it will transform not only how we trade, but how companies are listed. The role of the specialist will be similar to the roll of the upstairs prop desk. They will both offer capital for executions. It will be interesting to see how Corporate America will adopt to these changes.

MAHONEY: You need to think about consolidation not just in a traditional sense of physically moving people together and making big announcements. You can get a virtual consolidation in an electronic world, right? You used to need a supercomputer to solve complex problems. Now you can have a bunch of PCs linked together

---

[15] In 2005, the Financial Services Authority (FSA) in the U.K. adopted final rules on the use of soft dollars by FSA-regulated entities. Money managers could use client commission solely for the purchase of executions and research while non-permitted services had to be paid with hard dollars. The FSA also required managers to make timely and suitable disclosure of the arrangements to customers. The Securities and Exchange Commission, recognizing that money managers operate in a global market, considered the FSAs position in developing interpretative guidance on the Section 28(e) safe harbor that regulates soft dollars in the U.S. The interpretative guidance was approved by the SEC in July 2006. (The safe harbor was passed by Congress as an amendment to the Securities Exchange Act of 1934, shortly after May 1, 1975, when fixed commissions were abolished in the U.S. The safe harbor protects institutional investors when they pay more than the lowest available rate for research services.)

[16] As a result of the new guidelines in the U.K. a new soft dollar arrangement – Commission Sharing Arrangements (CSA) – gained a foothold there. CSAs allow money managers to pay executing brokers separately for trade executions and, at the same time, permit the manager to instruct the execution broker to allocate a portion of the commission directly to an independent research provider. A similar practice, known as Client Commission Arrangements (CCAs), soon gained traction in the U.S. In an No-Action Letter to Goldman Sachs in January 2007, the Securities and Exchange Commission formally made it clear that it would take no enforcement action in the case of a non-broker-dealer that received commission payments for its research services in a commission pool set apart in a "'client commission arrangement'" under Section 28(e) of the Exchange Act.

to solve the problem. So networks of exchanges will come together to let you have some sort of consolidation. In a post-NMS world, if you have order-protection, you effectively have some consolidated marketplace. So you have driven some consolidation into that.

BODINE: I will take a little different angle to that. Most of us feel more comfortable with the systems that we had available for the last 3 or 4 years. The one loss that I see happening is that both the buy-side and the sell-side historically have had an apprenticeship system to train new traders. It was always word of mouth, and someone would sit next to you. You would go through all this data and information. You would impart it to them, and in that way they would learn more about trading. When you felt comfortable, you would give them more and more to do.

Now we have an influx of technology. My head spins when I look at all the tools that we have. I do not know if I am really equipped to train the new traders any longer. I am not even sure what trading is anymore. The concern I have is that – well, it is probably a benefit for you, the academics – there is not a certification program out there for institutional buy-side traders. I do not know if there are any undergraduate programs with degrees in trading. There is a big void that needs to be filled with people who are competent with trading.

It used to be fairly straightforward and simplistic in terms of the goal. Now there are probably ten or 15 different areas each of us are responsible for. Five, ten, or fifteen years ago that was not the case. There is a potential loss of that apprenticeship system of training. But there are also people who can provide that education, which is a positive thing.

ROBERT SCHWARTZ [From the Floor]: I have to say something, George, about your call for education. There is much wisdom in that call. I would like to follow up and talk to you about it.

In terms of consolidation, the assertion made earlier is absolutely right. It does not mean that we are reduced trading to one floor, or to one spot. It could be virtual. But there are two dimensions to consolidation that I would like to put on the table. One is if you have different liquidity pools (be they dark or light or whatever shade of gray), but they are different and you link them. Is that the same as really having one liquidity pool?

The other thing that I would like to say is that, in the past couple years, we have started to talk, not just about price discovery, but also about quantity discovery. I have interacted with Paul Davis quite a bit on this. In fact, I thank him for focusing my attention on quantity discovery. But to a large extent (see if you agree with me) price discovery and quantity discovery have decoupled. Of course they cannot be harmonized the way they are in an economics textbook. But with greater consolidation of liquidity pools, wouldn't price discovery and quantity discovery be harmonized better?

UNIDENTIFIED SPEAKER: You just defined an exchange, didn't you? In effect that is the definition: in one place, you have quantity and price. We are all spending a lot of time and effort in the marketplace building systems that actually try to create some price discovery. But very little is done to define quantity discovery.

I was once at a meeting when somebody was asking what the next thing was that we had to build. Everybody else just talked about it in the context of the next block trade; the best quantity discovery. Nobody talked about the price. Nobody talks about the price because we know how to price. The problem is finding where the dead bodies are buried. That is tough. That is why we have fifteen different systems out there. They are all trying to find you the next block. It can be solved mathematically, optimally, but they were too complicated 5 years ago. There was actually a mathematical idea on how to do that. But they group with the idea were a bit like Lewis and Clark exploring the West. They had gone and found it, but people sill had to figure out how to do it. And, so far, I have not seen anybody coming out and doing it.

MAHONEY: I am sure that price and quantity discovery have always been decoupled, but you have had to seek them out separately. The last sale in block trading, for example, was always a reference point. You have always priced blocks at different prices than the retail price. We have probably become less accepting of it now.

Part of the reason you do not have more blocks now is that in a decimal world there are so many more price points. It is hard to sort of get your hands on where something should be priced and what the right discounts and premiums should be. You are resistant to that. In the eighth and quarter market (up a quarter, down a quarter, up a half, down a half) it was not a big deal. Now the cost of missing a single trade is generally a penny instead of twelve and a half cents, so you become less likely to trade. If it is now just a penny increment, you are only a penny away from the next trade. Let us not forget that.

UNIDENTIFIED SPEAKER: I will answer the first part of that question. You asked the following. If you have, say, two crossing networks and they come together, do you now basically have just one? We have always had fragmentation. The New York Stock Exchange was kind of a disguise in that they got all the credit for these prints. We may have negotiated upstairs with a Morgan Stanley or Merrill or Goldman. We may have agreed to a price, agreed to the quantity, and went to the NYSE to execute the trade. Then the specialist, or someone on the floor – that other black box – comes in, and all of a sudden you have aggregated a lot of size that was not there at the outset. So we have always had this fragmentation. But it was human fragmentation. Now we have electronic fragmentation. It has always been a part of the way in which we traded.

DAVID KRELL (International Securities Exchange) [From the Floor]: I was interested in your views of the countervailing needs of the portfolio managers versus the trading side and the buy-side. You guys represent the trading side, and obviously you are interested in the very fast, low-cost, low-impact trade. What about the portfolio manager who may be interested in research? How do you take care of those two different needs?

MAHONEY: You could do both. In the new world we ask, what is it that you pay? Who do you pay? Why do you pay for it? What can you do on your own? Then you work back from there. Traditionally, you would have paid a commission rate, and you would have expected certain things for it. Now that you are paying a different commission rate, generally lower, what are the goods and services that you need to receive from your brokers? Which brokers can provide them for you?

As I said earlier, a penny a share is only 4 basis points. That will not be the determinant of your success or failure. It is not what your client really wants. There are other factors involved such as the price and market impact costs. But you can do different things. If I can execute a greater majority of trades on my own, do I then pay a different rate than I would for a full-service where I would pay a higher rate? Yet the Goldmans and Morgans and Merrills of the world give us the different research services with this higher rate. That needs to be considered.

How often do I use these firms? When do I use their capital? When do I use their services? The entire process certainly has gotten more complex. One of the most interesting aspects of the FSA guidelines on soft dollars is that they mandate annual meetings between money managers and their top brokers to discuss the exchange of goods and services. What are you getting? What are you paying for? We are having that discussion here in the U.S. We are spending more time on that, but we do not want to be shortsighted. We do not want to say that we are looking to trade everything at a quarter of a penny because that is the right thing. We want to pay a reasonable rate for goods and services.

MURPHY: George wants that.

BODINE: We are not a fundamental shop, and we are not a totally quantitative shop either. We are a lot more process-driven. So in our shop, in our organization, the trader could do a lot of what the portfolio manager does because it is very systematic. By the same token, the portfolio manager can do a lot of what the trader does because you have these models that you are running. So we are closely aligned with how we process our particular orders for our style. If we were a more fundamental shop, the role of the trader and the portfolio manager would not be as aligned. Because trading is not as process driven.

MURPHY: Is there a risk with this change in the environment? Obviously, it is very different playing in the cash equity game today if you are not prop trading or in investment banking. How important is that? How many firms do you need to do business with? Times are pretty good. Still, we will hit a period, as we always do, when the margins are at the point where a lot of people will go away. There will be more consolidation within the brokerage business. By decompressing the commission rates, will you really motivate good people to stay in this business? Will you be able to compensate them? As things stand today, will we miss that idea from the broker? Are we driving this thing to mediocrity?

UNIDENTIFIED SPEAKER: If you are a good trader in a brokerage house, they will move you to the proprietary desk because that is where you will make more money.

UNIDENTIFIED SPEAKER: Correct. I want to work there. All of the good traders want to work there.

MAHONEY: They get paid more. The problem is that, if all the good traders become prop traders, the service that you will get from the non-prop guys will suffer. Will they really have any good ideas for you? Because if the ideas are good, you know, they will use them inside the house. You will find out that people are becoming more paranoid in this regard.

The point is, you do not want to let anybody outside know your ideas. This week has been interesting because the more brokers I have talked to, the more I realize that people are trading more proprietarily and putting in their own capital. Which they should do because they have to make money. They see that prop trading is performing well, so they put more money into it. The market participants who will lose are those who try without success to find professionals with ideas about trading.

MURPHY: One more question.

UNIDENTIFIED SPEAKER: Sometimes we get a bit myopic about what brokers are doing for us. We are still thinking in terms of single stocks. There are so many other alternatives today. The brokers are offering products such as swaps, and derivative products. Perhaps what brokers are losing on this commodity-type of single stock (and automated electronic delivery) product, they are recouping on all these swaps and structured products?

MURPHY: One more question, or comment. Anybody?

UNIDENTIFIED SPEAKER: Well, let's talk about outsourcing. It is not inconceivable that you could basically put a U.S. exchange on foreign soil. It is, after all, just a computer with some people to monitor to it. This is not farfetched. However, studies have also shown that if you try to extend trading hours or were going to trade IBM in China, that you won't generate a lot of participation from U.S. money managers. It is interesting that the Asian markets tend to wait until the U.S. markets open before they trade their securities. So the primary market will always capture the lion's share of the volume, at least while I am still working in this industry.

UNIDENTIFIED SPEAKER: As Tim mentioned, the top hundred stocks can easily be commoditized. You can easily outsource that part of the business. But when you get to mid-tier and that third-tier, it will be very difficult to do that.

UNIDENTIFIED SPEAKER: Also, in the U.S., mutual funds have single pricing based on the 4:00 p.m. close, Eastern Standard Time in the U.S. markets. So you must close the books on price at that time. Once you have a vehicle called the mutual fund that ends pricing at a pre-specified time, whether it is 4 o'clock or maybe 5, you have a defined moment in time in which you close the book and your prices. In this environment, it is tough to have a continuous market around the clock, 24-h-a-day.

UNIDENTIFIED SPEAKER: Maybe we have a radical side here, which is always trying to increase liquidity! How about if we were to shorten the trading day? Instead of trading for six and a half hours, maybe make it four, or four and a half hours. Obviously, if people need to get something done they will be more inclined to do that.

MURPHY: Cathy Kinney is speaking next, and I am sure that she will address that very topic. Thanks very much, panel.

Chapter 7
Dialog with Catherine Kinney

Catherine Kinney and Robert A. Schwartz

ROBERT A SCHWARTZ: I would like to welcome Cathy back. It is 2 years almost to the day that she was last here. It was an excellent keynote speech, despite the fact that she had a bad cold that day. The event ended with a wine reception and I had to lead her there by the hand (laughter). Are you feeling better now?

CATHERINE KINNEY: I am feeling very well.

SCHWARTZ: Excellent. As you know, we record the proceedings and turn the transcript into a book because we find the material valuable and want to keep it. But I have never found it more valuable than right now. Your speech from 2 years ago is in my book, and I went back and re-read it. In academia, we care a great deal about consistency so, with that in mind, can I quote you (laughter)?

KINNEY: Do I have a choice (laughter)?

SCHWARTZ: Probably not. At our conference in 2004 you said, "I will get started by recalling what Bill Donaldson said in a speech that he gave this past Sunday to the Society of American Business Editors and Writers in Fort Worth. It supports my opinion. Bill said, 'The leadership of our market depends on going to the benefits of technology while maintaining the advantages of the floor auction model for all investors.'" I presume you still agree with that?

KINNEY: Welcome to the hybrid market. I absolutely believe in that. Everything that we have been working toward on the exchange for the past year is unfolding, as we speak, on the floor of the New York Stock Exchange. We intend to succeed in providing the appropriate balance between human capital and intelligence, and excellent technology. We have been doing that, but we will certainly ramp up the technology side to provide faster (instantaneous) access, along with faster execution and anonymity for people who want that kind of execution.

We will also provide tools for the specialists and brokers to continue to interact with the auction. These new tools will be very responsive. They will give more choice to customers seeking to enter and exit the auction. The hybrid market is a visible statement that responds to that theme.

SCHWARTZ: I have long thought in terms of hybrids. It is clear that one size does not fit all, and that is why we need them. I have said over the years that a real strength of the NYSE is that it is a hybrid. You have long combined the agency

R.A. Schwartz et al. (eds.), *Competition in a Consolidating Environment*,
doi: 10.1007/978-0-387-75943-2_7, © Springer Science+Business Media, LLC 2008

market with the specialist who has the dual role of agent and dealer. You also have the call auction opening and the upstairs broker-dealer market. These things are very difficult to construct. You can call a market a hybrid, but it is also an ecology. It is an environment where different parts and participants co-exist, support each other, and feed each other. Your forthcoming structure is distinguished because, in your new hybrid market, H and M are capitalized. It is a hybrid that combines electronic and human components.

The exchanges in Europe are also hybrids. We started this morning with this view, largely from Europe. While I am saying this, I am looking at two of the survivors from this morning's session. England and France are sitting next to each other (laughter). We will drink wine together with them later. The NYSE, however, is introducing a kind of hybrid where, to put it differently, a slow market is being combined with a fast market. It must take a lot of thought to be able to accomplish this, to have it come effectively together.

KINNEY: It does take a lot of thought. Black boxes exist in lots of places. Many of you in this room work with one, send your orders to one, and get your executions from one. The challenging part of introducing the hybrid is meeting the commitments that we have made to our customers to deliver fast access, electronic execution and anonymity, while at the same time making sure that the professionals in the market can do their jobs effectively.

I am thinking about a broker representing a customer as an agent, and about a specialist providing liquidity for the stocks that need it. John Thain has gone on record saying that there are many stocks in markets around the world that can trade well electronically because they have a lot of liquidity. There is any number of stocks where you can count on a lot of buyers and sellers being capable of creating trades. But, in fact, the list of these stocks is actually very small. Get below that list, and it is apparent that stocks will trade better with provisional liquidity. And so we have a specialist on the New York floor. That is why we have been so successful for so long. We are able to create that liquidity. Even the Archipelago model provides a liquidity market maker in certain products.

SCHWARTZ: I have another quote.

KINNEY: Oh oh. Okay.

SCHWARTZ: I think that this quote applies to big stocks as well as to small ones. "That is the challenge," Cathy said, "to superimpose the auction in places where you need it at any moment." We tend to think of markets under normal conditions. In discussions, one always tends to think of what the average scene is like. For instance, when I go boating, what is Long Island Sound like on a reasonable day? But I have been out there when a squall has come up, and then, oh my goodness, you need structure. Roland Bellegarde and Nic Stuchfield, you have it in your exchanges. You need that structure. But Cathy, at the NYSE, you also turn to floor traders for the human element. You see, I do not only ask a question. I like to answer it too (laughter).

KINNEY: This gets back to the point you made earlier with respect to the fast and the slow market. I do not necessarily want to dwell on that dimension. I would like to say that the foundation and operating platforms of all markets today is technology. It is trying to make sure that technology is as efficient and cost-effective as possible. But there are moments when disruptions occur, either because of news, or because there are imbalances due to order sizes, or there simply are moments of insufficient liquidity when an auction is the best way to get information to customers and to create efficient price discovery. Our challenge, even in an NMS environment and the world we are headed to, is to balance these things so that we can continue to have auctions that deliver efficient price discovery. At the same time, we want to make sure that we are overlaying the technology that we know the marketplace needs. We need all of this to grow the cash equities business, at least for listed business. This is a challenge.

There are lots of tools though to meet the challenge. And the floor of the exchange will be an extremely vibrant part of how the market unfolds. This will be true even at much higher volume levels.

SCHWARTZ: I have another thought. We talk about dark liquidity and trades that could be made but aren't. The other side could well be out there, but how do you discover it? I am referring to the whole quantity discovery thing. There is also, and I get the term from Paris, "animateurs" (animators in English). Remember that term Roland? You do not call them that anymore, but it is the force in the hybrid that gets things going.

KINNEY: At the end of the day, people commit capital and take risks. Technology can certainly be programmed with algorithms to be more instructive in terms of decision-making. But ultimately it is people who do that. People write the programs, they write the algorithms, they take the risks, and they commit the capital. It is trying to use very efficient foundations with an overlay of intelligent systems and of people who take the risks and make the decisions. People need a lot of information to do that. Again, that is where technology plays an important role. It does so by disseminating, synthesizing and displaying information so that people can make decisions and take risks. I hope that with all of the technologies that we have, with the merger that we have created with Arca, with some new and exciting technology platforms, and the globalization that is inevitable, with all of these, I hope that we will have much deeper markets with a lot more technology to help us make decisions.

SCHWARTZ: It will be interesting to see how the animation role plays out in a more technologically computerized environment. (Why am I looking at David Krell while I say this?) There is more than one way to do it. Animation is a function of the people who bring orders together, get trades made, and have appropriate prices set.

I have another quote from you. "Everybody reminisces about the time when they could do a large block trade on the floor." Will those days ever come back? What might be done to encourage that? Do we want those days to come back?

KINNEY: We definitely want them back. People would like to do block trades. In some cases it is more efficient than slicing things up into little pieces. I like to call it death by a thousand cuts. People would very much like to do block trading again on the exchange.

Perhaps the most efficient way to get a block done today is to slice it up and use the systems where you get anonymity and efficiency. But it would be better to operate in a world with very liquid stocks on the floor of the exchange (say GE, Pfizer, or Lucent) where the bids and offers are deep, spreads are small, and the trading ranges are very tight. If you knew you could execute 250,000 shares instantly on the exchange through our systems, I believe that you would do so. I think blocks will return to the exchange as soon as people have the confidence and the certainty that they can get that execution done.

SCHWARTZ: Are there questions from the audience?

MARK FORZIATTI (Tudor Investments) [From the Floor]: Some critics of the hybrid say that the automation in this new market will generate a need for even more people on the floor. This is because of the proposed five-panels definition of the crowd for the broker entering an order on the floor into the reserve book.[1] We will be using people to get from point A to point B to transact an execution, rather than just hitting buttons on a terminal. I am curious about what your thoughts are.

KINNEY: Mark, the hybrid is about having choices. You will still have all of those choices to enter orders electronically into the marketplace. You will make choices about where an agent can be most efficient for you. The tools that we are giving the agents will make them more efficient than they are today. Whenever you transfer order flow to an agent, there are always some instructions, conversations, whatever, that go on in terms of developing a strategy for execution. The tools we are giving them will allow that to happen efficiently. The 5-panel rule is under review right now. Wherever you would consider the procedure inefficient, we want to make sure that those barriers make the procedure efficient. You will have the optimum number of choices in terms of how you will get an execution done, where you will get it done, and whether you get it done through a specialist, or by sending it directly to the point of sale, or by sending it to an agent. The end game here is to make everyone more efficient in the market. So, the scenario that you just described is not a problem but a solution. It should enable you to get your business done on the floor of the exchange.

ANTHONY FORTUNATO (Instinet, LLC)[2] [From the Floor]: I think that what Mark is trying to get at is, if I can put a discretion or reserve order in another

---

[1] Under the definition of the original hybrid, a floor broker who entered an order into the reserve book could not physically move more than five panels away from the panel at which he or she had entered an order. Failure to comply with this would result in an immediate order cancellation. The panels in question are the overhead electronic monitors that hang from the various trading posts on the NYSE floor. Each panel accounts for a group of stocks handled by a specialist. A later revision subsequently eliminated this "'five-contiguous panel'" definition of the "'crowd.'" The new definition instead divided each trading room of the floor into zones that established the boundaries of the crowd. Indeed, Kinney in her response at the conference, noted that the five-panel rule was then being re-examined.

[2] At the time of the conference, Mr. Fortunato was Director of U.S. Equity Sales and Trading at Nomura Securities International.

marketplace where the quote is protected, don't you want me to have the ability to send that order to the New York Stock Exchange without an intermediary who would make it less efficient for me?

KINNEY: We want you to send those orders to intermediaries because you think they add value. If you decide that that is not valuable to you, you will just put it in the system. You can do a reserve order from upstairs. Even today you do not necessarily need a system to do that. Our view at the moment is that the brokers add a lot of value. They need all the tools to continue to add value for you. We would like to see how that all plays out with those differences.

Remember, you will have automatic execution that you do not have today. You will have immediate or cancel capability for both market and limit orders, which you do not have today. You will have unlimited size (or at least 3 million shares worth in the very early going). It will be important to see how this unfolds. We think that is the right answer. Ultimately, you will decide whether we have gotten it right. And if we have not, we will continue to have a conversation with our customers.

SHANE FINEMORE (UBS Securities LLC) [From the Floor]: Can you give us some insight about any new experience you might need to change some of the rules with respect to access, to e-quotes upstairs, or to the disclosure of specialist volumes that are away from the quote. Posing the question slightly differently, if nobody used the e- quotes for the reasons that were just postulated, would you change it so that everyone would have open access to it? Would you get rid of the 5-panel rule and the floor broker environment?

KINNEY: We are trying to make the floor more efficient. The mission and the goal are to make sure that that auctions continue to run very efficiently with and for all of the players in it. If we conclude that participants need more tools to make it more efficient, then we will figure out what those tools are. With respect to the e-quotes, it seems to me, at least from the early experience, that there are a very large number of e- quotes done every day. I have actually been surprised. I think it is because the brokers across the floor now have the capability of putting in their own e-quotes. They are also able to use all of the tools that you are using upstairs – Dot, Direct + , everything. The experience has been very positive in terms of the efficiency of the broker.

There are clearly things that they would like us to improve on. We are working on fixing those things. Things like a d-quote [3] and pegging capabilities, which they will have in time for us to have full electronic execution. They will have all of those tools. We will see how things unfold. You can put a quotation in from upstairs by entering a limit order. You will have the ability from upstairs to put in an e-quote.

---

[3] D-Quotes are "discretionary" e-Quotes, which are electronic quotes used by brokers placing trading interest on a Display Book. Bids and offers are entered on hand-held devices at different prices in the crowd. D-Quotes may trade with any size contra interest; the floor broker may also establish a minimum and maximum size parameter, which dictates that the d-Quote is not permitted to trade with an order within that range, including at the minimum and maximum size established.

To address the earlier question, you will not have the reserve capability because we think that is best used by the brokers. Let us play it out and see how it goes.

UNIDENTIFIED SPEAKER [From the Floor]: I am a Baruch MBA student. I want to say thanks, we were at the exchange yesterday and it was a wonderful experience. We were talking to the NYSE technology group, SIAC, and also to the technology people with Archipelago. Can you speak a bit about the consolidation of those technology platforms?

KINNEY: We are working hard to integrate as much as we can so as to be more efficient. Many of you know in the context of the S-1[4] and things that we put out, that we must get more efficient in our business model. Technology will be one of the places where we can try to achieve some of the cost savings. That is number one. But with respect to features and services, Archipelago will continue to run its platform for its trading in NASDAQ securities. The New York Stock Exchange is very committed to the hybrid, and we will continue to go down the model for hybrid. Exchange traded funds are trading on two platforms today. We are looking at both of those to see which will be the more efficient model down the road. Those are areas where, on the execution side, models will be run independently, at least in the short term. We will use Archipelago in the fixed income market. As I said, we are using them in the exchange traded funds space.

One other development will be particularly useful for the broker-dealers. In 2007, we will have a common access point for both markets. If you are a firm today with lines into Arca and lines into the NYSE, you will have a common access point. You will be able to reach all of our products across a single access point. You will have the safety platform (the platform that we put in for reliability). It will be available for both complexes. Access to the entire portfolio of products through one common access point will be extremely efficient.

Then we will work on integration strategies in other areas. This summer we will get to another place that will be useful to us when we start doing automatic execution and the hybrid. One of the things embedded in autoex is auto routing and auto execution. It is in something that we call the NMS linkage. ITS will die with the introduction of the auto-ex and the hybrid. ITS will be replaced by the NMS linkage. Arca will start doing that for us at the end of the year. They will start doing front door access for us to other markets to reach out for liquidity. Dependence on linkages will be gone. Front door access will be the methodology. We will keep looking for every opportunity not to replicate things that they have already on their platform, and visa versa.

Arca is building capacity to back us up. We will get rid of many of the redundant data sites that we have. There are a lot of synergies, a lot of capability, and a lot of things that will be useful to the broker-dealers, as well as to those who access our market in terms of both cost and efficiency.

SCHWARTZ: I have a question that I have asked you before. Could you tell us what is happening with your opening and closing procedures and the call auction?

---

[4] Form S-1 is the document used to register securities with the SEC.

KINNEY: The opening and closing procedures are interesting because, in the hybrid market, we will still be using the centralized opening mechanism. We are not starting automatic execution until just after we open. But at the end of the day, the hybrid system will be going right up to 3:59 p.m. It will be interesting to see how that unfolds with regard to closing prices. We want the procedure to be efficient for all of the users. When participants most need to get to the close, we want them to be able to do so. But we also want to make sure that the pricing itself is efficient and well done. The opening and the close on the NYSE are probably two of the most efficient and liquid times in our trading day. This is something that the exchange does very well today. By and large, people want to make sure that that capability stays in tact. Once again, we will be using our tools (as many of them as we can), but we are constantly watching to make sure that we have not done something that is more disruptive or that is not helpful in integrating efficient price discovery.

SCHWARTZ: Any thoughts about intraday crosses?

KINNEY: Not at the moment. Arca has been doing that and has talked very openly about doing that. We keep talking to our partner about how to create some competitive capability, and we are very focused on not replicating things that they are doing, things that perhaps they can do more efficiently than we can.

SCHWARTZ: So, your answer is yes (laughter). I think of Arca as part of you.

KINNEY: They are. It is very interesting that you say that because people keep asking how the integration is going. I reply that we are tightly integrated already. The process has gone on for about a year. One thing that will be an important dimension is the transaction pricing that we were precluded from doing until the merger of the NYSE and Archipelago is completed.[5] That is something that we owe to the marketplace as a competitive matter. But it is also an important issue for the customers. We hope to be talking about that shortly.

SCHWARTZ: More questions?

UNIDENTIFIED SPEAKER [From the Floor]: You had mentioned that the hybrid and Arca are going to operate independently?

KINNEY: Yes.

UNIDENTIFIED SPEAKER [From the Floor]: Maybe I am just not aware of exactly how it will work, but if the hybrid and Arca are trading NYSE listed stocks at the same time, which I guess is conceivable, what would happen at times of stress

---

[5] The NYSE Group became the parent of the NYSE and Archipelago in March 2006 when the merger of both entities was completed. On June 30, 2006, NYSE Group announced new transaction-pricing changes for NYSE-listed equities and NYSE Arca traded options, effective August 1, 2006. This is what Catherine Kinney is referring to here. Prior to the merger, trading fees on the NYSE were paid by member organizations based on their level of trading activity. For example, fees were assessed on a per share basis in equity securities. These fees, which varied based on the size and type of trade, were charged on all transaction that occurred on the NYSE.

when the hybrid goes to a manual market? Will you have price discovery occurring simultaneously on both platforms? Is that a concern?

KINNEY: This is what will happen. We are basically sending a signal in a slow market that we think that price discovery needs to take place because there is going to be a significant price dislocation. As you know, under NMS rules, people will be able to trade through while we are slow. So Arca will continue to trade. It will be kind of business as usual. We will do what we think makes sense for our market and for the investors who have brought their orders to us. Hopefully we will do that in a way that adds value.

SCHWARTZ: Something that I am curious about is how your strategic thinking has changed since you have become for-profit. It is a different environment. Could you speak to that?

KINNEY: Sure. Three things have changed at the exchange from our perspective. One is governance, the second is the structure of trading, and the third is the strategy itself. With respect to governance, all of you know all of the changes that we made when John Reed came in. One very important governance issue is the construct of the public company that we have separated on the regulatory side. While I know that this has been a topic of a lot of discussion, we think that we have the right model. Our model keeps regulation just close enough so that it is knowledgeable and understands how the business is operating. That makes for the most effective regulation.

The second change, which is in the structure of trading, is something that we have been talking about in the hybrid. We are clearly moving down the road to more electronic execution, faster access, and greater anonymity. But it is a challenge to maintain the blend of what makes the exchange very special and at the same time retain all of the people who make that model work efficiently and effectively.

Regarding the third change, that of strategy, there are two important things. One is that we definitely see consolidation across the globe. John Thain has been very clear that he wants to have a leadership position in that consolidation. Second, multi-product platforms are the wave of the future both in and out of the U.S. You see that in a couple of ways. One is in the listing platforms, by creating a second listing brand for the exchange. Equally important is competing in more products than just cash equities (the model that we have had for many years). You will have an exposure to NASDAQ, an exposure to listed, to options, and to fixed income. All of you know we think that there will be an opportunity, in the options space, to trade options and cash side-by-side simultaneously.

There are a lot of opportunities. Bob, the title of this conference is very apt and appropriate to the timeframe that we are in: "Competition in a Consolidating Market." Competition will be global, it will be multi-asset class, and technology will be the foundation. Market structures will be very efficient. Hopefully, the consolidation will drive costs down for the users.

SCHWARTZ: My vested interest as an academician is to hear that the markets are remaining competitive. Having said that, I can add that I am totally in favor of competition because I have tenure (laughter).

UNIDENTIFIED SPEAKER [From the Floor]: You touched upon this in one of your first points, about the SRO. What headaches do you anticipate going forward? As an example, Arca, right now, has a lot of PCX rules. [6] Consider, for instance, the up-tick rule. [7] The NYSE has an uptick rule but there is none on Arca. How long is that going to take to normalize and standardize the rules?

KINNEY: I would need Rick Ketchum here to help me answer that. The regulatory side sits with him, and he is working to bring together the regulatory groups among the three players, Pacific, Arca and the NYSE. Some of those rules are specific to the products that they trade. Options has its set of rules, NASDAQ has its set of rules, and the NYSE and listed has its set of rules. There will not be a complete normalization or mutualization of the rule set. But the rules will be enforced and reviewed as appropriate to the product that is trading in a particular market. Rick will supervise the rules from a member firm perspective, from a market surveillance perspective, and from an enforcement perspective.

ERIC EXNER (Accenture) [From the Floor]: You mentioned that you want to play a role in global consolidation. I have two questions regarding this. Will you go for the London Stock Exchange? And if NASDAQ is faster than you are, what will your strategic response be?

SCHWARTZ: We only had time for one question, and that was it (laughter).

KINNEY: One good thing about being a public company is that, when you are in a quiet period, you can't answer that question (laughter).

SCHWARTZ: Al Berkeley?

ALFRED BERKELEY (Pipeline Trading Systems) [From the Floor]: Cathy would you take your NYSE hat off for a minute and talk about the trade reporting facility issue as it pertains to these businesses because it is very much in the news with NASDAQ's exchange listing.

KINNEY: We are very opposed to the trade reporting facility in terms of the direction it is headed in. Let me back up and explain that as part of the separation

---

[6] In 2005, the Pacific Exchange (PCX) was acquired by ArcaEx owner, Archipelago Holdings, which, in turn, was bought by the NYSE. As noted, in March 2006 the merger of the NYSE and Archipelago was completed when they became part of the NYSE Group. In late May 2006, soon after this conference, NYSE Group made a bid for Paris-based Euronext. In June 2006, NYSE Group announced it was buying Euronext in a $10 billion cash and shares offer. Finally, on April 2007, in ceremonies on both sides of the Atlantic, NYSE's takeover of Euronext – and the creation of NYSE Euronext, as the merged company is known – was consummated.

[7] The speaker is referring to the short sale "uptick rule" which required that stocks could only be sold short in an uptick. Arca had been exempt from the uptick rule. As part of the NYSE Group, the renamed NYSE Arca observed the uptick on the NYSE on securities not exempted. The SEC later voted to eliminate the short sale tick test, or "uptick rule" 17 CFR 240.10a-1 in all equity securities. Effective Friday, July 6, 2007, short sales on all securities were permitted on an up, down, or zero tick. (Back in July 2004, the SEC established a one-year pilot that temporarily suspended the tick test and short sale price test on any exchange or national securities association in certain securities. The agency later concluded that the uptick rule was no longer needed).

between the NASDAQ and the NASD, the NASD will have something called a trade reporting facility. Today, many of the broker-dealers in this room report their transaction to ACT and they get printed and credited to NASDAQ. In this separation, it is our view that those trades that are internalized within the broker-dealers should simply be reported to the NASD, and if in fact there is any market data credit or money or revenue generated, the NASD ought to keep that revenue and enhance their regulatory program. I think the SEC was supportive of this so I am not quite sure how it got disengaged – and that is that the market that played the role in price discovery ought to report and have credit for that transaction. If it was in fact an internalized trade in a broker-dealer's office, it should be reported to the NASD as an internalized trade. That is where it should end.

We have been extremely vocal about this and the reason is two fold. One, you hear NASDAQ talk repeatedly about their growing market share in a number of venues including ours. Much of that growth is completely reported trades. And two, this is a very large revenue opportunity for NASDAQ. If people continue to report to ACT in this separated environment it is probably about a $25 million benefit to NASDAQ. Our view is that the NASD should keep the trades. If revenue accrues to it, they should keep the revenue and use it for a regulatory program.

We could argue another dimension of this which is that we should not encourage more internalization because that is a very pernicious thing. It is not good for markets. I am sure we could have a great debate with a lot of people in this room on that topic. I think it encourages more internalization which is not healthy for the concentration of liquidity in markets. More importantly, a lot of competition is centered around economics, but it is also centered around information. The information ought to be associated with the place of price discovery, not with the place of reporting.

SCHWARTZ: Very interesting. Cathy I can't tell you how happy I am about your having been here. It was very informative and we thank you very much (applause).

Chapter 8
Life After the Big Board Goes Electronic[1]

Paul Davis, Michael S. Pagano, and Robert Schwartz

For over 200 years, change has come slowly at the New York Stock Exchange. By the turn of the twenty-first century, much electronic technology for handling orders and information had been introduced but the Big Board's basic, floor-based trading structure was still intact. Today, trading remains centered at the posts of specialists who have an affirmative obligation to make fair and orderly markets, and who manage the limit order books (generally small orders). Intermediate-sized orders are routinely handled by floor traders, and large orders negotiated in the upstairs offices of the broker/dealer firms are commonly brought to the floor to be executed. Intermediaries (specialists and other floor traders) play a key role in making trades and, for large and mid-sized buy and sell orders, only minimal use is being made of the computer at the most critical point in the exchange process – when orders meet and are translated into trades.

But much of this is now changing. In the Spring of 2006, the NYSE reached a turning point marked by the development and partial rollout of its "Hybrid Market," a carefully designed, complex system that combines two major components – the traditional floor-based facility (referred to as a "slow market") and an electronic platform (referred to as a "fast market"). The slow market is desirable because of its ability to offer price improvement for market orders and special order handling for large orders, and the fast market has value because of its ability to offer speed, anonymity, and customer control. Thus, the Hybrid Market is designed to combine the traditional NYSE trading floor functions of the specialist and floor brokers with an electronic order book that contains automatic execution capabilities.

If successful, the Hybrid Market will combine the best of two worlds – the stability of a slow, intermediated market and the speed and certainty of a fast market.[2] When the dust settles on this market structure innovation, some anticipate

---

[1] Davis, P., Pagano, M. and Schwartz, R., 'Life After the Big Board Goes Electronic,' *Financial Analysts Journal,* volume 62, Number 5, September/October 2006, pp. 14–20. Copyright 2006, CFA Institute. Reproduced and republished from Financial Analysts Journal with permission from CFA Institute. All rights reserved.

[2] For more details on this new market innovation, see John Thain's description of the Hybrid Market in Schwartz et al. (2006, Chap. 2) and at the NYSE web site (www.nyse.com).

R.A. Schwartz et al. (eds.), *Competition in a Consolidating Environment,*
doi: 10.1007/978-0-387-75943-2_8, © Springer Science+Business Media, LLC 2008

that orders for big cap stocks will go predominantly to the fast electronic market, and that orders for the smaller issues will go predominantly to the slow, floor-based market. We address the question of where trades go when an exchange's main trading platform is electronic.

The success of the Hybrid Market may not be known for some time. At this stage, what might one expect? To address some of the broader issues involved, we discuss the operations of the current NYSE floor-based system that provides price discovery and quantity discovery, albeit less than perfectly. We also raise several key questions: How will the electronic, fast market component affect the operations of the NYSE's current network? If floor activity is lessened or ceases to be, will more order flow be executed in the broker-dealer houses and alternative trading systems?

Floor-based trading has largely been eliminated in the major European equity markets. An example is London's Big Bang in October 1986 when the London Stock Exchange launched its SEAQ screen. A quote from a floor trader, Anthony Abrahams, underscores the speed with which this change can occur: "Within five minutes of Big Bang on Monday morning it was clear to me that the floor was dead. I am not bragging. I was the last person in the City to figure it out!" (see Clemons and Weber, 1990).

How successful are the electronic markets for the non-blue chip stocks and, for all market cap sizes, for handling the big orders of large investors? We present evidence for one European country (Germany) that the electronic order book, while the recipient of substantial order flow, is only one venue that traders use to meet their objectives. This finding is an important indication of what life may be like in the United States after the market adjusts to the Big Board's fast market innovation.[3] It suggests that a reasonable balance between the use of fast and slow market technology may be achieved.

Price Discovery, Quantity Discovery, and Network Effects

Equity markets must meet the changing needs of different classes of market participants. We consider the equity marketplace primarily through the lens of buy-side institutions and their intermediation needs. We are not ignoring the small participants since many retail customers rely on buy-side institutions for their equity investments.

Size is the overriding distinction between institutional orders and retail orders. For large institutional orders, we refer to the size of an order for a single name (a 1,000,000 share order for a liquid stock is not unusual), and to the size of a basket

---

[3] We should also note that there are substantial differences in the regulatory environment and market structures of the NYSE and German equity markets. Thus, our analysis does not represent a direct, apples-to-apples comparison and should be interpreted with appropriate caution.

order (there can be 1,000 names in a basket with an average order size of 1,000 shares.) Equity market structure must facilitate the efficient execution of both single name orders and basket orders. There is an important distinction between a 1,000 share retail order for a stock and a 1,000 share institutional order that is part of a basket trade – the basket order will likely be laced with contingencies (e.g., a maximum net dollar difference between purchases and sales may be stipulated). Electronic trading is essential for the efficient handling of basket orders; this is not necessarily the case for large, single stock trades.

Recognizing the complexities of order handling, the enormous differences between a 1,000 share retail order, a 1,000,000 single share institutional order, and a 1,000,000 share basket order, and given the varying trader needs for speed, anonymity and control, the challenges facing market architects and government regulators who oversee the markets are enormous. To achieve desired answers, two fundamental goals for the broad market must be kept in focus: sufficiently accurate price discovery and reasonably complete quantity discovery.

Price discovery refers to finding the price that best reflects the underlying desire of participants to buy and sell shares. A well-discovered price could be considered an equilibrium (or consensus) value. Because equilibrium prices are not observable before trades are made, and given that all orders are not submitted simultaneously, finding an equilibrium value is a complex, dynamic process.[4] The prices that we actually see in a market reflect the orders that participants submit, the structure of the market that determines how orders are handled and translated into trades, and the size of the market (e.g., the number of participants and/or market cap). The market's structure and size establish the network. Taking a market's structure as given, larger markets are expected to deliver better price discovery.

Quantity discovery involves participants disclosing their orders so that they can meet each other and transact the total number of shares that they wish to buy or to sell. Ideally, price and quantity discovery should go hand-in-hand, much as in any microeconomics course the simultaneous solution for price and quantity is given by the intersection of a demand curve and a supply curve. In real world equity markets, however, quantity discovery is rarely simultaneously achieved with price discovery, nor is it generally complete.[5] That is, contra-side orders that could in principle meet and trade with each other are commonly held in participants' pockets and not disclosed to the market. This is true especially for big orders that are not fully revealed because participants fear market impact. For a given market structure, larger markets are expected to deliver more complete quantity discovery.

---

[4] For further discussion of the dynamics of price discovery, see Paroush et al., Schwartz, and Wolf (2006).

[5] See Moulton (2005) for further discussion of investors' desire to trade at specific quantities and the increased price impact of trading at precise quantities, particularly by institutional investors at the end of a calendar quarter.

To date, the Big Board continues to receive a bit more than 70% of the order flow for its listed stocks.[6] The NYSE's architecture consists of both a "fast" component (the SuperDot system and Direct+) and a "slow" component (the floor traders and specialists on the floor of the exchange). The new Hybrid Market restructuring will change many of the features of the NYSE, but it will hopefully preserve a vibrant network that offers both fast and slow trade execution.

Why not go to a fast market only? A purely electronic order driven platform is certainly compelling. It is cheaper to operate, and it offers speed, anonymity, and control.[7] Perhaps the reason it does not dominate is that a slow market, in some situations, actually is not slow. That is, matching a large buy and sell order in a single trade may accelerate the execution of the entire package. "Slicing and dicing" (the usual characterization of large orders being executed in smaller pieces over an extended period of time) is highly prevalent in today's marketplace. Each tranche of a large order can receive a fast execution, but the procedure may nevertheless be slow for the entire order.

The bottom line is, for a market to be an effective network, a fast electronic component cannot do it all. For large orders in particular, improper order handling can lead to sizable market impact costs and, by offering more intelligent direction, the human tortoise can outpace the electronic hare.[8] And so intermediation will retain its importance irrespective of the existence of an electronic platform. But the form that it might take is not easily foretold. At this time, just how the introduction of the NYSE's fast market will change the balance between order book trading, floor trading, and the upstairs market is not very predictable. If the floor survives, the distribution of the order flow will be determined by competitive forces but, if the profitability of floor trader operations erodes to the point where the floor trader firms cease their operations, the floor could collapse. If so, the network efficiency of the Exchange will be profoundly affected.

The reality is that price and quantity discovery have already partially decoupled in the current environment. For the most part, prices of NYSE-listed shares are discovered on the Big Board's trading floor, an environment where relatively small, retail orders play an important role. As we have noted, larger, hard-to-work orders may be sliced and diced and brought to the floor over extended sequences of trades; they may also be executed in an NYSE call auction or off-board, either in the upstairs market, in a crossing network, or in a block trading facility. Consequently, while price discovery largely occurs at the Exchange, quantity discovery increasingly does not.

---

[6] The percent received by the NYSE, in December 2005, was 73.25%. See NYSE Facts & Figures web site (formerly known as the NYSE Fact Book) at http://www.nysedata.com/nysedata/Default. aspx?tabid = 115.

[7] In a fast market only environment, the role of the floor broker passes to brokers who work orders electronically. These agents would not necessarily be affiliated with the NYSE.

[8] See Boehmer (2005) for further discussion and analysis of the trade-off between differences in the speed and cost of trading on an electronic system versus a floor-based market. Overall, the author finds a positive relation between the speed and execution cost associated with a trade.

It is possible that the bifurcation between order book-provided price discovery and off-book-provided quantity discovery will sharpen. On the other hand, if the NYSE's new market structure better facilitates the handling of large orders, the two processes may be brought into closer harmony. Before attempting to peer into the future, let us first take a broad look at off-exchange trading and then obtain some perspective on the current importance of fast market, order book trading at one exchange, Germany's Deutsche Börse, where the primary focus is on electronic trading.

Off-Exchange Trading

Institutional orders that by-pass the NYSE, for the most part, are executed in the upstairs markets of broker-dealer firms or on alternative trading systems. Trades made in the upstairs market occur when customer orders are executed against broker-dealer capital (referred to as "internalization") or are matched against each other (referred to as netting). Regional exchanges are often used to print netted trades and, traditionally, these exchanges have been used to internalize retail order flow.

The informal view of participants with whom we have spoken is that an appreciable proportion of institutional order flow (roughly 40% or more) by-passes the electronic book trading platforms of exchanges in the United Kingdom, Germany, and Canada.[9] The informal opinions about order flow diversion are reinforced by the success that alternative trading systems have had in the U.S. in recent years. These systems include crossing networks such as ITG's Posit and two block trading facilities, Liquidnet and Pipeline. For NYSE, Amex, and Nasdaq shares, current daily trading volume is in the neighborhood of 30 million shares for Posit, 40 million shares for Liquidnet, and 15 million shares for Pipeline, and their volumes are growing.[10] Like brokers who internalize, these alternative trading systems take order flow away from the exchanges.

Evidence on the Prevalence of Order Book Trading in a Fast Market Environment

Of primary interest regarding the NYSE's Hybrid Market is the amount of order flow that will be directed to its fast market component. To gain more insight into the prevalence of order book trading in an electronic environment, we have assessed

---

[9] The diversion does not appear to be as substantial in Paris, in part because France has an order concentration rule which requires that orders be brought to the Euronext Paris platform for execution.

[10] Trading volume for these alternative trading systems are 'double counted,' meaning that each share traded is counted twice (as one share bought plus one share sold).

the division of the order flow between trades that go through an exchange's order book (on-book trading) and trades that by-pass the book (off-book trading) for one other country, Germany. The German order book data include trades made on Germany's physical trading floors, but Deutsche Börse's main trading platform is electronic, and on-book trading is predominantly fast market activity directed to the Exchange's Xetra system.

Currently, there is no trade reporting requirement in Germany and, consequently, the actual amount of off-book trading (and even off-board trading) in German stocks has not been known. Our approach to estimating the importance of on-book trading should conservatively be viewed as a "best guess effort." It involves the use of Cascade settlement instructions data from Clearstream, the major settlement service provider for German stocks.

On-book trading in Germany offers speed and strict time and price priorities. But participants have alternatives, and we emphasize that the on-book market share (the metric that we focus on) is not a measure of Deutsche Börse's overall market share. Orders can be sent directly to Xetra (an on-book order), or can be reported directly to the clearing and settlement system (an off-book order), or can be entered through Xontro, the Exchange's electronic order routing system that offers both on- and off-book entries for normal-sized orders and block trading. There are no specific block trading arrangements on the Xetra order book, no trade-through rule that prevents a block from executing outside the spread, and no requirement that a block trade be printed.

Deutsche Börse has provided us with monthly order book trading volume for 160 actively traded stocks on the Deutsche Börse, as well as a proxy for off-order book activity obtained from the Clearstream settlement instructions (with all broker and customer identifications suppressed) for two evaluation periods: the month of January 2006, and July 2003 through June 2005.[11] The Cascade settlement instructions include entries that are non-trade related position shifts which, fortunately, for the most part, are not included in our data.[12] We have employed an (albeit imperfect) way of assessing the magnitude of any potential double counting of trades and, as will be discussed below, conclude that it is not substantial enough to unduly distort our conclusions regarding the division between on-book and off-book trading.[13]

Our measure of on-book trading is to some extent more accurate. As noted, it includes all trading on Deutsche Börse's electronic trading system, Xetra, and on various physical trading floors (primarily in Frankfurt and, to a far lesser extent, in Munich and other German exchanges).

---

[11] Special thanks to Robert Urtheil and Miroslav Budimir of the Deutsche Börse for making these data available to us.

[12] Regarding non-trade related position shifts, reliable estimates are not available, but anecdotal evidence suggests that securities lending and repurchase transactions are very small compared to aggregate OTC trading volume. Additional details on non-trade related position shifts are available from the authors upon request.

[13] More details on the specific algorithm used in the present analysis are available from the authors upon request.

We assess the relative magnitude of order book trading using both value-weighted and equally weighted averages across all stocks in our sample. The value-weighted average reflects the division between on-book and off-book trading for the representative euro value of trading. The equally weighted average reflects this division for the representative firm. We present statistics for both averages but, because the value-weighted average is heavily influenced by a relatively small number of firms with large trading volumes, we direct our attention mainly to the equally weighted average.

Exhibit 8.1 shows, for the month of January 2006, the percentage of the euro value of trades that goes through the order book for the 160 companies that comprise four major German stock indexes (denoted as "All 160" in the graphs), and for the stocks in each of the indexes: the 30 DAX large cap stocks, the 50 mid cap MDAX stocks, the 50 small cap SDAX stocks, and the 30 TECDAX technology stocks. The euro value-weighted market share statistics are displayed: (1) using the adjustment procedure noted above to eliminate double counting, and (2) based on the "raw," unadjusted Cascade data.

We see in Exhibit 8.1 that the value-weighted averages for adjusted on-book activity are uniformly higher than the value-weighted averages for the unadjusted data – the percentage point differences range from 3 to 10 (43% vs 40% for SDAX stocks and 49% vs 39% for DAX stocks). This is not surprising given that the adjusted data are explicitly intended to eliminate the double accounting of trades associated with OTC dealer operations. For both the adjusted and unadjusted measures, the on-book market share is similar for the DAX, MDAX, and SDAX stocks, and roughly 20 percentage points higher for the TECDAX stocks.

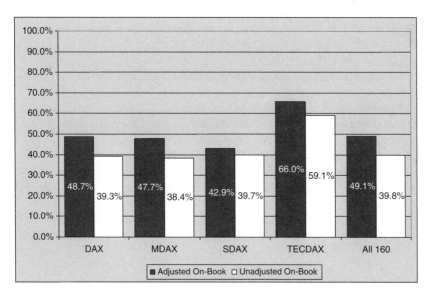

Exhibit 8.1 January 2006 German On-Book Market Share by Trading Volume in Euros (value-weighted, both adjusted and unadjusted)

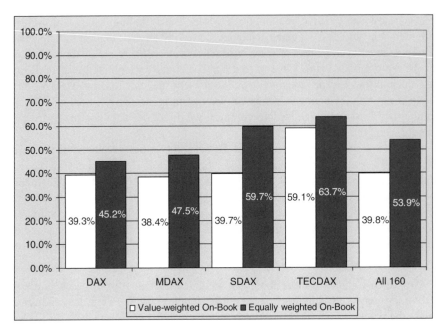

Exhibit 8.2 January 2006 German Unadjusted On-Book Market Share by Trading Volume in Euros (both value-weighted and equally weighted), in terms of Cascade Settlement Volume

While our adjustment procedure may help correct the over-statement of off-book trading, the value-weighted averages may be excessively influenced by a relatively small number of heavily traded stocks. To assess this possibility, in Exhibit 8.2, we contrast the value-weighted and equally weighted averages for the unadjusted data. All of the equally weighted on-book trading averages are higher than the comparable value-weighted averages. For all 160 stocks, the equally weighted average is 54%, while the value-weighted average is 40%. This contrast suggests that off-book trading is more prevalent for the larger, more actively traded stocks.

The on-book market share averages for both the adjusted and unadjusted data, and for both the equally weighted and volume weighted averages, range from 38% to 60% (with the exception of the stocks in the TECDAX index, for which the on-book averages are between 59% and 66%). Overall, our four different ways of assessing the percentage of on-book trading portray a roughly consistent picture. It appears from the January 2006 data that a reasonable market share estimate for order book trading in Germany is 50%.[14]

But data for just one month may be noisy. Accordingly, in Exhibit 8.3, we further report equally weighted averages for the 2-year sample period (July 2003–June 2005)

---

[14] The relatively high on-exchange TECDAX market share might have been inflated by some non-recurring trading activity in a particular sub-sector of technology stocks during January 2006.

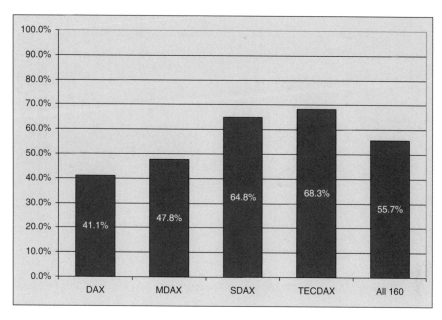

Exhibit 8.3 July 2003–June 2005 German Unadjusted, Equally Weighted On-Book Market Share by Trading Volume in Euros, in terms of Cascade Settlement Volume

based on unadjusted data. In so doing, we are implicitly assuming that data adjustments for the longer period would be relatively small, as they are for January 2006.[15] In Exhibit 8.3, the finding for "All 160 Stocks" of 56% is virtually the same as the comparable equally weighted average of 54% shown in Exhibit 8.2 for January 2006. But, in contrast with Exhibit 8.1 and 8.2, the 160-firm aggregate statistic in Exhibit 8.3 masks considerable variation across the four major German stock indexes. Over the 2-year period, for the 30 large cap DAX stocks only 41% of euro volume occurred on-book, while a more substantial 68% of trading in the smaller TECDAX stocks was on the book.

Across the four indexes, Exhibit 8.3 reveals a clear size-based difference between on-book and off-book trading percentages that is implicit in the relationship between the simple and value-weighted averages shown in Exhibit 8.1 and 8.2. Larger cap stocks trade more heavily off the book, roughly half (48%) of mid-cap volume goes through the book, and a clear majority (65%) of smaller cap stocks trading goes through the book.

Our finding that larger stocks experience more off-book trading is reasonable. Large institutional investors, who are typically more active in the larger cap issues, are less likely to direct their block orders to the book, and retail orders for the larger cap stocks are more likely to be netted and internalized by German banks and brokers.

---

[15] Adjusted data are not available for the two2-year sample.

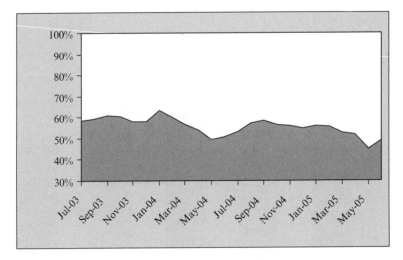

Exhibit 8.4 Time Variation in Unadjusted, Equally Weighted Market Share of all 160 Stocks during July 2003–June 2005 (by Trading Volume in Shares), in terms of Cascade Settlement Volume

Turning to how the market share of on-book trading has changed over time in Germany, Exhibit 8.4 shows how the unadjusted, equally weighted average statistics for all 160 stocks has varied over our 24-month sample period. The graph displays substantial variation in the statistics over time, with the on-book market share hitting a peak of 63% in January 2004 before falling to a low of 45% in May 2005. For the 2-year sample period, the monthly on-book market share had a standard deviation of 4% around its mean of 56%. No particularly meaningful trend is evident in the data shown in Exhibit 8.4.

Overall, Exhibit 8.1–8.4 show that, over an extended period, off-book trading accounts for a very substantial portion of trading in a major country's equities. Of course, this pattern could, in part, be attributable to Germany's unique market structure, regulatory environment, and history. Nevertheless, our findings suggest that a further investigation of off-book trading in an electronic environment would be desirable.

Our Foggy Crystal Ball

Dramatic technology advances, powerful regulatory pressure, and intense intermarket competition have united to exert a virtually unstoppable force for the NYSE to introduce a new electronic platform of its own. All else constant, this development represents a dramatic step forward for the Exchange. But all else will not be constant, and consequences are not easily predicted.

If the components of the hybrid operate effectively together, they will offer valuable choices to participants. But will they co-exist successfully? Will the flow of orders to the fast market components of the NYSE and other fast markets seriously erode floor trader profitability? If so, the floor could disappear and market quality for the smaller issues could deteriorate. The SEC's new trade-through rule, which disallows transactions that "trade through" the best posted quotes (highest bids and lowest offers), will substantially level the playing field for fast market competitors.[16] Given the positive obligations of specialists that are not shared by non-exchange competitors, will the NYSE find itself at a competitive disadvantage as a fast market post-Regulation NMS (the regulation that contains the trade-through rule)?

Our crystal ball is indeed foggy but, in broad scope, this is the picture that we see. While we do not attempt to be a soothsayer with regard to merger outcomes or regulatory consequences, we do know that there will be fast market competitors for the 1,000 share orders (whether these orders are retail, a part of a basket, or a slice of a larger block). We have viewed the wide ranging NYSE network as producing two services of overriding importance: price and quantity discovery; without question, introduction of the Hybrid Market will impact the operations of this network. We have assessed the magnitude of on-book trading in Germany, where an electronic platform is dominant. The reassuring news for the Hybrid Market is that trading in Germany is split roughly 50–50 between on-book and off-book despite the fact that this national market offers a state-of-the-art, electronic trading platform. Interestingly, the on-book market share appears to be smaller for the large cap stocks, which suggests that the fast market component of Hybrid Market may not be overly dominant for the NYSE blue chips, and that the slower, floor-based component can continue to fulfill an important function. This is consistent with an opinion expressed by William Donaldson in 2004: "The leadership of our market depends on going to the benefits of technology while maintaining the advantages of the floor auction model for all investors."[17]

A word of caution: if the fast market component of the Big Board's new Hybrid Market lessens floor activity or, in the extreme, results in the floor shutting down, many large orders will migrate elsewhere. The role of the floor broker will pass to agents who "slice and dice" and trade electronically as they do now for NASDAQ-listed names. We expect that the search for natural liquidity would then lead to considerably more order flow being internalized and netted in the broker-dealer houses, and/or directed to alternative trading systems. As harbingers of change,

---

[16] The rule was originally scheduled to go into effect in 2006, but has been delayed until late 2007.

[17] Donaldson was previously CEO of the NYSE and Chairman of the Securities and Exchange Commission. The quote from his speech, delivered on May 2, 2004 to the Society of American Business Editors and Writers in Fort Worth, was presented by Catherine Kinney at a May 4, 2004 conference at Baruch College in New York. The transcript is contained in Schwartz et al. (2006).

block trading systems and crossing networks are increasingly gaining market share. And so, one thing is easy to see in our foggy crystal ball: competition between the NYSE, the upstairs market, and the alternative trading systems will remain intense for a long time to come.

Acknowledgments We thank Miroslav Budimir, Rainer Riess, Martin Reck, and Jamie Selway for their assistance and comments on an earlier draft of this paper. We are also grateful to an anonymous referee and the editor, Rodney Sullivan, for additional useful comments.

References

Boehmer, E. 2005. 'Dimensions of Execution Quality: Recent Evidence for U.S. Equity Markets.' *Journal of Financial Economics* vol. 78, no. 3 (December), 553–582.

Clemons, E.K., and B.W. Weber. 1990. 'London's Big Bang: A Case Study of Information Technology, Competitive Impact, and Organizational Change.' *Journal of Management Information Systems*, vol. 6, no. 4 (Spring), 41–60.

Moulton, P.C. 2005. 'You Can't Always Get What You Want: Trade-Size Clustering and Quantity Choice in Liquidity.' *Journal of Financial Economics*, vol. 78. no. 1 (October), 89–119.

Paroush, J., R.A. Schwartz, and A. Wolf. 2006. 'Trading, Price Setting and Volatility in Equity Markets Under Divergent Expectations and Adaptive Valuations.' Working paper, Baruch College.

Sarkar, A., and R.A. Schwartz. 2005. 'Two-Sided Markets and Inter-Temporal Trade Clustering.' Working paper, Baruch College.

Schwartz, R.A., J. A. Byrne, and A. Colaninno. 2006. *Electronic Vs. Floor Based Trading.* Springer Science + Business Media, Inc.

Schwartz, R.A., R. Francioni, and B. Weber. 2006. *The Equity Trader Course,* John Wiley & Sons.

Participant Biographies

Brooke Allen is the head of the Quantitative Trading Group at Maple Securities in Jersey City, NJ. At the time of the conference, Mr. Allen was with MANE Fund Management, Inc.

Doug Atkin is President and CEO of Majestic Research. He was previously President and CEO of Instinet Group, where he conducted the IPO (NASDAQ: INGP), developed Instinet's research, international trading and correspondent clearing businesses, and led a consortium of nine global brokerage firms that took a majority stake in the virt-x stock exchange. Doug serves as a member of the Board of Directors of Starmine, WR Hambrecht, Investorside and Tamale Software, and has been named twice to *Institutional Investor* magazine's Online Finance 30 annual ranking of the most important leaders in international e-finance. He is a graduate of Tufts University.

Roland Bellegarde is deputy CEO of the Euronext global cash markets, responsible for all aspects (operating the NSC trading system, product development and member relations). Roland holds an advanced studies degree in Economics, Finance and Banking from the University de Paris II Sorbonne. During the course of his career at Paris Bourse (since 1986) and Euronext, he has acquired a great deal of international experience in the development of electronic trading systems for the exchange. He defined the functionalities of the NSC trading systems which currently operates on all Euronext markets. Roland has been leading the process to integrate the NSC trading platform across the Euronext markets and has as such defined and developed the global Euronext market model for securities trading. Roland gained international authority for his in-depth understanding of the global markets. He is spearheading the taskforce for Euronext regarding its positioning in these markets. Roland is fluent in English and French and has extensive contacts at senior level with global banks and understands their trading objectives. An understanding of regulatory and legal requirements is core to his day to day management of the Euronext cash market activities. Roland is seen as an experienced pragmatic person with a high level of authority, whose amicable and interpersonal approach is highly regarded by the market players and by his Euronext team.

Al Berkeley has over 30 years of experience in the financial industry. Prior to joining Pipeline, from June 1996 until August 2003, Al served as President and then Vice-Chairman of The Nasdaq Stock Market, Inc. Before Nasdaq, Al was a Managing Director of Alex. Brown & Sons, a leading investment bank. Al co-founded Alex. Brown's Technology Group in 1975. The Technology Group completed about 500 financial offerings for clients while he was associated with the Alex. Brown. Al is a graduate of the Wharton School of Finance of the University of Pennsylvania (MBA) and the University of Virginia (BA). He served as an officer in the United States Air Force.

George H. Bodine is currently Director of Trading for General Motors Investment Management Corporation (GMIMCo). He is responsible for worldwide equity and derivative trading relating to GMIMCo's internal investment funds. Prior to assuming his current position in September, 1996, Mr. Bodine was Vice President of Schwab Institutional overseeing equities and options trading for the small to mid-tier investment advisors. Preceding that, he spent his career with Equitable/Alliance Capital starting in 1972. Mr. Bodine received his BS in Psychology in 1972 from Syracuse University and MS in Business Management in 1979 from Central Michigan University. Mr. Bodine is currently a member of the Securities Trader Association and National Organization of Investment Professionals. He is a former member of both the NYSE and AMEX Institutional Traders Advisory Committees. He is on the Advisory Board of the Ballentine Investment Institute at the M. J. Whitman School of Management at Syracuse University.

At the time of the conference, **Mike Cormack** was an Executive Vice President of the NYSE Group, Inc. Mr. Cormack was responsible for managing new product initiatives for the NYSE Group in addition to the equity trading business of NYSE Arca and ArcaEdge, an OTCBB trading platform. Prior to its merger with the New York Stock in March 2006, Mr. Cormack was President of Archipelago Holdings, Inc., the parent company of the Archipelago Exchange (ArcaEx). In that role, Mr. Cormack oversaw client relation efforts including sales, trading support, and strategic initiatives. Prior to his position as president, Mr. Cormack served as National Sales Manager. He came to Archipelago from American Century Investments where he was manager of Equity Trading. Mr. Cormack has a strong background in both trading and technology. His technical experience is exemplified by his prior position as co-head of the executive committee for the Financial Information Exchange (FIX) – an emerging electronic communications standard in the global financial marketplace. He has also participated as a member of the Nasdaq Quality of Markets Committee, a group that helps to shape Nasdaq policy. He currently serves on the board of Recovery Point Systems. Mr. Cormack holds a bachelor's degree in economics from The Johns Hopkins University.

Noreen M. Culhane, executive vice president, Global Corporate Client Group, for the New York Stock Exchange, is responsible for the Exchange's worldwide efforts to attract new listings and to serve companies already listed. Ms. Culhane manages Business Development, Client Service, Marketing and Sales Support functions, the

Initial Public Offering process and Structured Products for the Exchange's business worldwide. Before joining the NYSE, Ms. Culhane spent 20 years at IBM, most recently as the Business Unit Executive for the securities industry. Her responsibilities in this position included sales, services and relationship management for major domestic securities firms. Ms. Culhane serves on the Management Committee for the NYSE and is a member of the Economic Club of New York. She also serves on the Fund Raising Board of the Borough of Manhattan Community College as well as the Board of the College of Mt. St. Vincent, her alma mater. Ms. Culhane has a graduate degree in Education from the College of New Rochelle and completed the Advanced Management Program at Harvard.

Paul Davis retired from TIAA-CREF in February of 2006. He served as a senior managing director, as head of trading and as co-head of quantitative portfolio management. He continues at TIAA-CREF in a part time capacity working on special projects. He has an undergraduate degree from West Virginia University and a doctorate in mathematics from Carnegie Mellon University. Before beginning his Wall Street career, he taught mathematics at the university level. Along with more customary retirement pursuits, he is writing papers with Professors Robert Schwartz and Mike Pagano as well as planning a new business enterprise that introduces a new (and better) way to evaluate the investment process.

Alfred Eskandar is Director of Corporate Strategy at Liquidnet. He is responsible for Liquidnet's strategic initiatives and new business opportunities. Prior to joining Liquidnet in 2000, Alfred helped launch Securities Industry News, which was acquired by Thomson Financial Services in 1996. From 1996 to 2000, Alfred was the head of business development for the operations, trading and technology division and developed an international executive conferences business for Thompson Financial's Investment Marketing Group. Alfred has 10 years of financial media experience and holds a BBA in Finance and Economics from Baruch College.

Eric Exner is partner in Accenture's strategy practice with more than 10 years of consulting experience in financial services with a focus on capital markets. Mr. Exner is program director for the Accenture Capital Markets Industry Group in Europe, Asia and Latin America. He has deep knowledge about strategy development as well as business and operating models for financial institutions, focusing on investment banks and exchanges. His specialty are business and operating models as well as finance, accounting and controlling. Mr. Exner graduated from Universität Karlsruhe (TH) as "Diplom-Wirtschaftsmathematiker." He also holds an MBA from INSEAD (Fontainebleau) with a focus on Corporate Finance and Banking.

Luca Filippa is the Director of Research and Development at Borsa Italiana and the Chairman of the Economics and Statistics Committee of FESE (the Federation of European Securities Exchanges). He is also a member of the Advisory Group on Statistics of the World Federation of Exchanges. After 5 years in the Economic Research Dept. of Consob (the Italian Securities Commission), he moved to Borsa Italiana, holding different positions of increasing responsibility in the areas of economics, statistics and taxation. He is a lecturer of Market Microstructure at the Università Cattolica of Milan and author of articles and papers on equity markets, securities industry, financial taxation and household savings. He takes part as speaker in conferences on Exchange industry evolution, market microstructure, tax policy and XBRL.

Mr. Finemore is a Former Managing Director and Head of the U.S. Fundamental Investment Group at UBS Investment Bank. He is a formerly a member of the UBS Investment Bank Board, U.S. Equities Operating Committee, and co-chaired the U.S. Equities Trading Committee. He had spent 17 years with UBS Investment Bank and its predecessor firms as Head of Australasian Equities and Head of Trading for Australia. Prior to that, he was Risk Manager and Market Maker in Equity, Index, and Interest Rate Derivatives at Dominguez Barry Samuel Montague, where he began his career in 1990. Mr. Finemore was Chairman of the Australian Financial Markets Association's Equity Derivatives Committee from 1999 to 2001. He is currently a board member of the Australian Securities Exchange and is a CFA charter holder. Mr. Finemore has a B.Comm from the University of New South Wales.

Mark Forziati is a senior vice president at Tudor Investment Corporation. Mark has been with Tudor since 1993, when Tudor started the Boston Equity division. He served as a member of the NYSE ITAC committee from 1991 until 1993. In 1997 he was invited to speak before a congressional sub-committee on decimalization of stock prices, an issue he pushed for as a member of the NYSE ITAC committee.

Reto Francioni has been Chief Executive Officer of Deutsche Börse AG since 1 November 2005. From April 2002 to October 2005 Reto Francioni was Chairman and President of the SWX Swiss Exchange. Prior to assuming this post, he was co-CEO of Consors Discount Broker AG, Nuremberg. Earlier in his career, he was named in 1993 to the board of Deutsche Börse AG, where he was responsible for its entire cash market division and, as of 1999, became Deputy CEO. Reto Francioni studied law in Zurich where he also earned his PhD in law. He held different management positions in the securities exchange and banking sectors of Switzerland and the USA, as well as in the directorate the corporate finance division of Hofmann LaRoche AG, Basle. He is a professor for applied capital markets theory at the University of Basle, as well as member of the International Advisory Board of Instituto de Empresa, Madrid. Publications: "Equity Markets in Action," (Wiley 2004, Robert A. Schwartz and Reto Francioni) and "The Equity Trader Course" (Wiley 2006, Robert A. Schwartz, Bruce W. Weber and Reto Francioni).

Prof. William C. Freund is Professor Emeritus and Director of the Freund Center for the Study of Securities Markets, Pace University.

Mark A Guillaumier joined the Malta Stock Exchange in 1992 becoming CEO in 2001. After graduating in economics at the University of Malta he worked for a commercial bank before moving to the Central Bank of Malta as Head of Money and Banking and Advisor on Monetary Policy. During this period he was seconded to the International Monetary Fund in Washington DC where he gained experience in Financial Programming for Developing Economies. Mark is currently Chairman of the Steering Committee on Clearing and Settlement in Malta and Advisor to the Malta Ministry of Finance. He also represents the Maltese Government in a number of EU Committees in Brussels.

David Harris is CEO of the CBOE Stock Exchange. At the time of the conference, he served as The American Stock Exchange's Senior Vice President of Business Planning and Strategy where he was responsible for planning and implementing critical aspects of the Exchange's strategic direction, including developing strategic relationships with other markets, developing future market structure, and providing guidance regarding business development and other initiatives of importance to the Amex and its customers. Prior to joining the Amex, Mr. Harris served as Executive Vice President and General Counsel of Nasdaq Liffe Markets LLC (NQLX), formerly a joint venture between The Nasdaq Stock Market Inc. and the London Financial Futures and Options Exchange. Mr. Harris was a founder of NQLX and played a vital role in planning, directing, and executing the exchange's successful launch and subsequent operation. Mr. Harris has also served as Counsel to Chairman and Chief Executive Officers of the NASD and Nasdaq. Earlier in his career, Mr. Harris served as a Senior Associate at Kirkpatrick & Lockhart and as Senior Counsel in the Division of Enforcement at the Securities and Exchange Commission.

William R. Harts is Managing Director and Head of Strategy for Equities at Banc of America Securities (BAS) and is responsible for electronic trading services strategy and product development, including algorithmic and quantitative strategies, as well as oversight of the design, integration and deployment of technology across the Equities platform. He is well known as a pioneer of automated market making and algorithmic trading as well as an authority on financial market structure and applied technology.

Marcus Hooper develops and implements trading technologies for the Global Electronic Trading Solutions team at Bear Stearns International. For 17 years prior to this Marcus traded and managed trading desks for major asset management firms, including the Investment Management divisions of HBOS, Dresdner and AXA. He has been actively involved in industry committees and advisory groups looking at Financial Markets regulation, market structure, transaction cost analysis and the application of electronic trading technology. Marcus has provided input and direction to projects carried out by organisations including the Investment Managers' Association, The British Bankers' Association, The London Investment Banking Association, The FSA, The European Commission, The London Stock Exchange and FIX Protocol Limited. He has published papers on Financial Markets Behavior, including studies of best execution methodologies, electronic and alternative trading systems and transaction cost analysis. Marcus is proud to have been a nominated speaker for AIMR's educational program.

Brian Hyndman is Senior Vice President of NASDAQ's Transaction Services. In this capacity, Mr. Hyndman is responsible for managing the day-to-day operations of the transaction services area. As Senior Vice President of NASDAQ Transaction Services, he is also responsible for the broker/dealer sales and the institutional outreach and relationship program. Mr. Hyndman played a key role in the acquisition of INET and is currently managing the integration of the sales team and customer relations. In addition, he has helped lead the launch and implementation of new products and programs such as the Opening Cross, Listed program, and other initiatives to leverage the Brut ECN asset. Mr. Hyndman guided Brut's growth since its founding. Appointed President of The BRASS Utility in April 1998, Brian presided over the company's merger with Strike Technologies in February 2000, the subsequent formation of The Brut ECN, and SunGard's acquisition of Brut in August of 2002. Brian then presided over the sale of BRUT to Nasdaq in September of 2004 and worked on the integration of BRUT into Nasdaq. Prior to joining Brut, Mr. Hyndman served as Vice President of Execution Services for the National Discount Brokers Group, managing 120 employees. He holds a Bachelor of Arts degree in Psychology from the State University of New York at Oswego. He also holds numerous licenses from the National Association of Securities Dealers, including the 4, 7, 24, 27, 53 and 63.

Catherine R. Kinney is president and co-chief operating officer, NYSE Group, Inc. In this role, she is responsible for overseeing the relationships with member firms and institutions, the listings business, NYSE market operations and the Hybrid project. Prior to her current position, Mrs. Kinney was president and co-chief operating officer of the New York Stock Exchange. Prior to that position, she was group executive vice president of the New York Stock Exchange since June 1995. Prior to that, since 1986, Mrs. Kinney was responsible for managing trading-floor operations and technology. Mrs. Kinney joining the NYSE in 1974 and rose through the ranks, holding management positions in several divisions, including Technology Planning, Sales and Marketing, and Regulation. She is a member of the boards of the NYSE foundation, Depository Trust & Clearing Corporation (DTCC), Georgetown University, Junior Achievement of New York, U.S. India Business Council, and Catholic Charities. She served on the Board of the Metropolitan Life Insurance Co. from 2002–2004. Mrs. Kinney graduated Magna Cum Laude from Iona College and completed the Advanced Management Program, Harvard Graduate School of Business. She has received honorary degrees from Georgetown University and Rosemont College.

Susanne Kloess is Partner at Accenture and is based in Munich. Working since 1988 for Accenture mainly in the Financial Services Industry operating group, she has been responsible for large-scale projects in the Capital Markets Industry in Europe, Asia and the US. Her specific expertise includes electronic trading systems in the securities and derivatives markets as well as clearing and settlement and investment banking. She played a lead role in many projects Accenture delivered for various exchanges and alternative trading systems in Europe, Asia and the US. Ms. Kloess heads the Capital Markets Group of Accenture in Core

Europe. She is also managing partner of Accenture's business in the German and Austrian Banking market.

David Krell is a founder and President & CEO of ISE. From 1997 to 1998, he was Chairman and co-founder of K-Squared Research, LLC, a financial services consulting firm. From 1984 to 1997, Mr. Krell was Vice President, Options and Index Products, of the New York Stock Exchange where he managed marketing, systems and new product introductions for the division. From 1981 to 1984, Mr. Krell was First Vice President at the Chicago Board Options Exchange, responsible for the management and operation of the Marketing and Sales Division. Mr. Krell was also a Vice President of Merrill Lynch from 1978 to 1981 and founded its Managed Options Service. Mr. Krell is active in numerous industry groups. He was a Director on the Board of the International Federation of Technical Analysts, a president of the Market Technicians Association and a Director on the Board of The Options Clearing Corporation. Mr. Krell formerly was an Adjunct Professor at Rutgers University Graduate School of Management and at the Graduate School of Baruch College. He has taught, coordinated and directed numerous seminars and workshops at the New York Institute of Finance.

John W. Labuszewski is Managing Director of Research & Product Development at the Chicago Mercantile Exchange where he is responsible for the Exchange's product development efforts. Before coming to the CME in 1998, Mr. Labuszewski was General Manager of Nikko International's U.S. Asset Management Division where he was responsible for the development and operation of managed futures and hedge funds. He has also worked for Virginia Trading Company, a subsidiary of Kleinwort Benson; Refco, Inc. and the Chicago Board of Trade. Mr. Labuszewski is the author of four books on financial markets including Investing in Government Securities: Fundamental and Technical Analysis, Portfolio Management and Arbitrage, John Wiley & Sons, 1994 (w/ Frederick Barnett & Dennis Heskel); Trading Options on Futures: Markets, Methods, Strategies & Tactics, John Wiley & Sons, 1988 (w/ John E. Nyhoff); Trading Financial Futures: Markets, Methods, Strategies & Tactics, John Wiley & Sons, 1988 (w/ Nyhoff); and, Inside the Commodity Option Markets, John Wiley & Sons, 1985 (w/ Jeanne Sinquefield). He has written numerous articles for Journals including the Financial Analysts Journal and other trade and industry publications. He earned an MBA from the University of Illinois in 1978.

Tim Mahoney is currently with BIDS Trading. At the time of the conference, he was Head of Equity Trading at Merrill Lynch Investment Management. He joined MLIM in August of 2000 where he managed 14 traders for the Equity Funds Group which operates a 24-h global trading desk in Princeton. He began his career with Merrill Lynch in 1979 and held a variety of positions in the firm's Defined Asset Funds division including Head of Equity and Fixed Income Trading and Chief Investment Officer. He has an undergraduate degree from the College of the Holy Cross and a MBA from the Stern School of Business at New York University. He is also a CFA.

At the time of the conference, **John McGonegal** was Senior Vice President, Equties at the American Stock Exchange. Mr. McGonegal managed the equity sales, issuer services, research and equity order flow functions at the Amex. He played an integral role in increasing the Amex's presence within the venture capital, investment banking and business communities, while focusing on the acquisition and retention of Amex company listings. Prior to joining the Amex in 2002, Mr. McGonegal was at Quick & Reilly for 10 years, where, in his most recent position, he was branch manager at Quick & Reilly's largest U.S. branch office network. He held various positions in trading, sales and management. Mr. McGonegal received a bachelor's degree from the State University of New York at Buffalo. He has his series 4 (options principal), 7, 8, 63 and 65 licenses. He also holds the CMFC designation from the College of Financial Planning, and is a former NCAA basketball player. He was recently named one of Irish America magazines Wall Street 50 for 2003.

Michael Murphy is President and Founder of Piney Run Capital LLC, a financial service firm located in Baltimore, Maryland. Previously he was head of Equity Training at Wachovia Securities. Prior to joining Wachovia, Mr. Murphy was a founding partner of Kern Capital Management, where he was Director of Trading. He has also been Director of Trading at Morgan Grenfell Capital Management and Partner at Alex Brown & Sons where he headed up Sales Trading. Mr. Murphy has served on a variety of industry committees including the Upstairs Traders Advisory Committee at the NYSE, the Institutional Trader's Advisory Committee at the NYSE, the NASD'S Institutional Committee and the Investment Company Institutes Institutional Trading Committee. He is also a member of NOIP. Mr. Murphy is viewed as an expert on market structure issues and is a frequent speaker at industry conferences. He was educated at West Virginia University and resides in Baltimore.

William O'Brien is Senior Vice President, New Listings in the Corporate Client Group of The Nasdaq Stock Market, Inc. In this position Mr. O'Brien is responsible for managing the Nasdaq's efforts to deliver the benefits of Nasdaq's superior market structure and value-added services to prospective listed companies. Prior to his current role, Mr. O'Brien was Senior Vice President of Market Data Distribution, responsible for the sales, management and business direction of Nasdaq's real-time and historical market data business. Prior to his tenure at Nasdaq, Mr. O'Brien was Chief Operating Officer of Brut, LLC. As COO, Mr. O'Brien participated in the management of all, strategic, operational and administrative affairs of the company, and helped lead the company through its acquisition by Nasdaq in September 2004. Mr. O'Brien originally joined Brut as Senior Vice President and General Counsel in September 2000, with responsibilities that included management of Brut's legal affairs, regulatory strategy and compliance area. Previously, Mr. O'Brien was Vice President and Assistant General Counsel at Goldman, Sachs & Co., where he was responsible for providing legal coverage to the firm's prime brokerage, stock loan, equity finance, equity operations and soft-dollar business units. Before joining Goldman Sachs he was an Associate at Orrick, Herrington & Sutcliffe LLP, practicing in their Market Regulation Practice

Group and working with a variety of broker-dealer clients, including the operators of electronic communication networks and other alternative trading systems. Mr. O'Brien graduated cum laude from both the University of Notre Dame and the University of Pennsylvania School of Law.

Michael S. Pagano is an Associate Professor of Finance at Villanova University. Professor Pagano has conducted several empirical analyses related to various issues in market microstructure, financial institution management, risk management, cost of capital estimation, and interest rate determination. He has published in numerous finance journals such as the Journal of Financial Economics, Journal of Banking and Finance, Journal of Portfolio Management, and the Financial Analysts Journal. In addition to serving on the editorial boards of two academic journals, Professor Pagano has been a Fulbright Scholar at the University of Costa Rica and has received awards for both teaching and academic scholarship. Prior to earning his doctorate and joining the Villanova University faculty, Professor Pagano spent over 10 years in the financial services industry. He holds the Chartered Financial Analyst (CFA®) designation and has experience both in commercial lending activities at Citibank and in investment valuation analysis at a financial consulting firm, International Capital Markets Corp., as well as Reuters PLC. In addition to his duties at Villanova University, Professor Pagano has been a consultant to several companies including Citibank, PaineWebber, Fidelity Investments, GTE Investments, Philadelphia Suburban Corp., Aqua America, and Bank Julius Baer.

Bob Pisani is *On-Air Stocks Editor* at CNBC. A correspondent since 1990, Bob Pisani has covered real estate and corporate management, and now reports on Wall Street from the floor of the New York Stock Exchange. He was nominated twice for a CableACE Award, in 1993 and 1995. Prior to joining CNBC, Pisani co-authored "Investing in Land: How to be a Successful Developer." He also taught real estate development at the Wharton School of Business at The University of Pennsylvania for 5 years with his father. Pisani learned the real estate business from his father, Ralph Pisani, a retired real estate developer.

Martin Reck started his career as Assistant to the Executive Board of Deutsche Börse AG in 1993 and became Head of the Xetra Market Model Development Team in 1995. From 1997 till 1998 he was Inhouse Consultant IT/O at Deutsche Bank AG. In 1998 he returned to Deutsche Börse AG as Head of Market Design and Functionality Xetra. In 1999 he took the project lead of Deutsche Börse's e-commerce initiative and became CEO of Xlaunch AG in 2000. Since January 2003, he is also Managing Director of Deutsche Börse AG and Head of Group Functionality. Martin Reck holds a Ph.D. in Information Systems of the Institute for Information Systems, University of St. Gallen.

Jim Ross is Vice President of NYSE MatchPoint and oversees the development and operations of NYSE's equity crossing business. Jim is also deeply involved with organizing NYSE's broader ATS strategy. Prior to joining NYSE in July of 2006, Jim was CEO of MatchPoint Trading, a firm dedicated to the business of electronic call market trading. From 1989–2003, Jim spearheaded Instinet's Global

Crossing business; most notably building its daily U.S.equity crossing business, establishing its international crossing business, launching JapanCross,the first Japanese equity crossing service, as well as the first multi-currency, UK, VWAP and FX crosses. Jim also oversaw global institutional sales at Instinet from 2001–2003. With over 18 years of management and operational experience in the electronic crossing industry, Jim is a frequent conference panelist and contributor to articles and papers about crossing networks and dark pools. When he is not criss-CROSSING America, he is in Connecticut with his wife, Victoria and two children Olivia and Emmett.

Mony Rueven is Managing Director at D.E. Shaw & Co. Prior to re-joining D.E. Shaw Mony Rueven, was Knight Capital Group Senior Management Director, Head of the Broker-Dealer Group. Mony is a veteran of equity risk management and proprietary trading with more than 20 years of experience in building automated trading systems. He joined Knight in April 2003 to oversee the company's newly-created Electronic Trading team. Before joining Knight, Mony was President of Springline Capital, LLC, a statistical arbitrage hedge fund where he developed and managed sophisticated trading technology. Prior to that, he was a Managing Director and Head of U.S. Enhanced Portfolio Strategies at BNP CooperNeff. From 1994 to 2000, Mr. Rueven was a Managing Director of D.E. Shaw & Co. Mony came to D.E. Shaw from Credit Suisse First Boston where, from 1992 to 1994, he worked to add major corporations and money management firms to the company's client base for equity basket trading. Mony has also served as Managing Director for Jefferies & Co.'s Investment Technology Group (ITG) and Thomson Financial Services, where he managed the ALERT Group and developed their OASYS global automated account allocation system.

Robert A. Schwartz is Marvin M. Speiser Professor of Finance and University Distinguished Professor in the Zicklin School of Business, Baruch College, CUNY. Before joining the Baruch faculty in 1997, he was Professor of Finance and Economics and Yamaichi Faculty Fellow at New York University's Leonard N. Stern School of Business, where he had been a member of the faculty since 1965. Professor Schwartz received his Ph.D. in Economics from Columbia University. His research is in the area of financial economics, with a primary focus on the structure of securities markets. He has published over 50 refereed journal articles and fifteen books, including *The Equity Trader Course* (co-authored with Reto Francioni and Bruce Weber) Wiley & Sons, 2006, *Equity Markets in Action: The Fundamentals of Liquidity, Market Structure and Trading* (co-authored with Reto Francioni) Wiley & Sons, 2004, and *Reshaping the Equity Markets: A Guide for the 1990s,* Harper Business, 1991 (reissued by Business One Irwin, 1993). He has served as a consultant to various market centers including the New York Stock Exchange, the American Stock Exchange, Nasdaq, the London Stock Exchange, Instinet, the Arizona Stock Exchange, Deutsche Börse, and the Bolsa Mexicana. From April 1983 to April 1988, he was an associate editor of The Journal of Finance, and he is currently an associate editor of the Review of Quantitative Finance and Accounting, the Review of Pacific Basin Financial Markets and Policies, and The

Journal of Entrepreneurial Finance & Business Ventures, and is a member of the advisory boards of International Finance and The Journal of Trading. In December 1995, Professor Schwartz was named the first chairman of Nasdaq's Economic Advisory Board, and he served on the EAB until Spring 1999. He is developer, with Bruce Weber, of the trading and market structure simulation, TraderEx (http://www.etraderex.com/).

Jamie Selway is Chairman and Managing Director of White Cap Trading LLC, a brokerage firm located in New York. Jamie and his partners founded White Cap to provide institutional investors with cost-effective, unconflicted brokerage. White Cap accomplishes this through an agency-only approach and an expertise in electronic markets. In addition, White Cap offers insight on the changing structure of marketplaces, so that its clients are well-positioned to maximize execution quality and minimize information leakage. Before forming White Cap, Jamie was Chief Economist at Archipelago Holdings, LLC, the Chicago-based electronic brokerage firm and creator of the first totally open, fully electronic U.S. stock exchange. Jamie served a variety of functions at Archipelago, including strategy, quantitative research, regulatory and governmental liaison, and new business development.

Jamie's other professional experiences include the Equity Derivatives Research group of Goldman, Sachs & Co. (New York), 3 years in the Economic Research group at the National Association of Securities Dealers, Inc. (Washington), and 2 years at Economists, Inc. (Washington). Jamie has written articles published in both industry press and academic journals, and has been quoted in the Wall Street Journal and the Financial Times. He currently serves on the Users Subcommittee of the Intermarket Trading System and as an Associate Editor of the Journal of Trading. Jamie holds an M.S. in Financial Mathematics from the University of Chicago and a B.A. in Mathematics and European History from Washington & Lee University, Phi Beta Kappa.

George Sofianos is Vice President, Goldman Sachs, Equity Execution Strategies. He joined Goldman Sachs in 2001 and he is leading the firm's trading cost and market structure analysis effort for equities. Prior to joining Goldman Sachs, he was Head of Research at the New York Stock Exchange. Before joining the NYSE, he worked at the Federal Reserve Bank of New York, in the Financial Studies department and at the Open Markets Desk. He began his career teaching finance at the Stern Graduate School of Business, New York University. Mr. Sofianos has published research on execution strategy, trading costs, market structure, the cross-listing and trading of non-U.S. stocks, the NYSE specialist trading behavior, stock price behavior on expirations, the impact of program trading on intraday stock price volatility, and index arbitrage. He holds B.Sc and M.Sc. degrees from the London School of Economics and received his Ph.D. in economics from Harvard University. Mr. Sofianos is a Practitioner Director of the Financial Management Association (FMA) and an Associate Editor of the Journal of Trading.

Nic Stuchfield is Director of Corporate Development, an area that includes Strategy, Research and Business Planning. Until 2006, he was also Managing

Director of EDX London, which is a joint venture derivatives exchange between the London Stock Exchange and OMX. Nic joined the Exchange in August 2003 from The Stuchfield Consultancy. Prior to that, his roles included spells as CEO of Tradepoint (now Virt-x), COO of Barclays Global Investors and COO & CFO of BZW's global equities business. EDX London is a Recognised Investment Exchange ("RIE").

Larry Tabb is the Founder and CEO of The TABB Group, an advisory firm focused on helping financial services firms, vendors, and technology integrators better understand, create and execute their technology visions. Subsequent to its founding in May 2003, The TABB Group has worked on helping both the large (global investment banks) and the small (new technology start-ups) better plan, articulate, and hone their technology and business strategies. The TABB Group has also worked to provide industry insight through seminar series and research on algorithmic and electronic trading, the future of trading technologies, and grid computing in financial markets. Larry is also a contributing editor for Wall Street and Technology where his monthly Perspectives column discusses technology issues germane to the global securities industry and a frequent contributor to FinExtra.com an industry website dedicated to informing the global financial services industry key breaking issues where his Tabb on Technology column discusses issues of the day. Prior to founding The TABB Group, Larry was the Vice President of TowerGroup's Securities & Investments Practice where he managed research across the Capital Markets, Investment Management, Retail Brokerage, and Wealth Management segments. Larry was the founding member of TowerGroup's securities and investments business and instrumental in growing the business into a global brand representing over 150 research clients around the world. Larry has published research analyzing ECNs; electronic bond trading systems; fixed income, equity, and foreign exchange trading systems; back-office trade processing systems; broker workstations; analytical trading tools; infrastructure development tools; and foreign and emerging market technologies. He has also written extensively on new technology trends in straight-through processing, cost management, and advances in emerging technologies. Quoted extensively and in virtually all industry and general news publications, Larry has been citied in The Wall Street Journal, CNN, Bloomberg, CNBC, Reuters, Dow Jones News, Barron's, Wall Street & Technology, Securities Industry News, Waters, Computerworld, American Banker, The Banker, and Information Week. He has also been a featured speaker at numerous industry conferences such as the SIA's Annual Meeting, and the SIA Technology Management Conference. He has talked on topics such as straight-through processing, wealth management, financial planning, business continuity, and overall technology trends in securities. Larry was the driving force and author of technology surveys cosponsored by TowerGroup and the Securities Industry Association (published biennially): Technology Trends in the Securities Industry: Investing in Tomorrow's Infrastructure, 2001 and Technology Trends in the Securities Industry: Transition to an Online World, 1999. He was coauthor of the 1997 Technology Trends in the Securities Industry: Spending, Strategies, Challenges, & Change. These are in-depth analyses of technology trends and spending within the securities industry that have been widely distributed and quoted. Prior to joining TowerGroup, Larry managed business analysis for Lehman Brothers' Trading Services Division and was responsible for overseeing the specification, testing, and implantation of dozens of major systems during his tenure. Larry was also in charge of capital markets technology planning at Lehman Brothers where he developed the 1 and 3 year technology plans from 1988 through 1992.

Larry began his career managing various operations for the North American Investment Bank of Citibank, he managed the front-office trading operations, the front-office finance operations and various back-office money market operations. Larry culminated his 6 year Citibank career when he managed Citibank's Proprietary Trading clearance and settlement operations for U.S.Treasury Debt.

Mark Wright is a Managing Director responsible for global product management at ITG. He joined ITG as Vice President of software development in 1990 and has held several roles including Manager of the software development organization for ITG and Chief Information Officer. Prior to joining ITG, Mr. Wright was a Director of software development at Inference Corporation. Mr. Wright has a degree in computer science from Carnegie Mellon University.

Index

A

Advanced Execution Service (AES) for Credit Suisse, 81
AIM stock market, as competitor, 50
Alternative trading systems, 55, 59, 65
American stock exchange
    electronic trading and, 24–25
Archipelago trading platforms, 33
Atkin, D., 22–23, 25–26, 28–29, 33–34, 36

B

Balog, S., 4
Banc of America's InstaQuote platform, 56
Bellegarde, R., 10–14, 18–19, 90
Berkeley, A., 53, 57, 60, 64, 66, 67, 97
Big Board's fast market innovation, 100
Bodine, G., 70, 71
Broker/dealers (BDs), 55
    internal crossing engines for, 62
    services and offerings by, 61

C

Calvin, D., 14
Capital pricing, 81
Cascade settlement volume
    instructions data from Clearstream, 104
    time variation in unadjusted, equally
        weighted market share, 108
Cedar Creek Management, 4
Central Securities Depository, (CSD), 18
Chicago Mercantile Exchange (CME)
    business model, 35–36
        production monopoly, 24
    listings and, 41
    pillars of, 41
    vertical structure, 17
Clearstream settlement instructions, 104
Client Commission Arrangements (CCAs), 83

Commission compression, 71
Commission Sharing Arrangements (CSA)
    and soft dollar arrangement, 83
Cormack, M., 23, 26–28, 31, 33
Culhane, N., 37, 42, 45–47, 50–52

D

Daimler-Chrysler merger and trading, 20
Davis, P., 4
DAX large cap stocks, 105
Deutsche BÖrse
    electronic trading and, 103–104
    euronext and, 1–2, 34
    for German shares, 57
    overall market share, 104
    vertical integration, 35
Direct market access (DMA) products, 33

E

Eastern Standard Time in U.S. markets, 87
Equilibrium prices, 101
Equity markets and participants,
        100–101
Eskandar, A., 21–22, 26, 30–32, 35
Euro, 59. *See also* European capital market
    dollar futures contract, 48
    Eurex and, 5
    value of trading, 105
Euronext
    clearinghouse and, 18
    exchange structures, collapse, 11
    regulators of, 11
European capital market
    blue chips, 57
    equity markets, 59
    exchange industry, 59
    investment banking community, 57
Exchange Traded Funds (ETFs), 40

F

Fidelity/Lehman Brothers
    announcement, 76
Filippa, L, 53, 57, 59
Financial Services Authority (FSA) in U.K.
    and soft dollars usage, 83
Finemore, S., 93
Floor-based trading, 100
Fortunato, A., 77, 92
Forziatti, M., 92
Francioni, R., 1–5
Freund, W., 18–19
Friedman, T., 72
Friedman, T. L., 3, 72
FSA guidelines on soft dollars, 86

G

Germany
    on-book market share by trading volume
        in euros, 105
    order book data, 104
    stock indexes, 105
    unadjusted, equally weighted on-book
        market share by trading volume
        in euros, 107
    unadjusted on-book market share by
        trading volume in euros, 106
Global equity market and changes
    algorithmic trading and, 7–8
    best execution, 14
    cross-border complexity, 18
    customer relations management, 15–16
    data centers, 12
    European markets, 18–19
    German and U.S. traders, 20
    governmental structure, 16
    growth potential, 8–9
    hybrid markets and, 12
    instruments, volume increase, 7
    investment banks, 15
    IT based–technology, 10
    off-book trades, 13
    reconcile block trading, 9–10
    regulators, role, 10–11
    single markets, 12–13
    vertical and horizontal structures, 17
Global Winds of Change, 7
Goldman Sachs Execution and Clearing
    (GESC), 60
    program desk for, 61
Goldman Sachs REDIPlus products, 71
Gresack, M., 19
Guillaumier, M., 10, 17

H

Harris, D, 24, 29, 35
Harts, B., 46
Harts, W., 53, 55–57, 59–62, 64–68
Hooper, M., 9, 14, 19
Hybrid Market, 89, 99–100, 109
    centralized opening mechanism in, 95
Hyndman, B., 23, 28–30, 32

I

Indian stock markets, 58
Information technology
    liquidity and fragmented pools in, 65
    switching costs of, 4
Inter-market trading system, 14
    competition and listing decisions
        brand and, 45
        under covered companies, 47
        ETFs and, 44
        financial futures and, 41
        horizontal and vertical integration, 35
        listed companies meeting, 43
        media coverage, 42–43
        NASDAQ and, 39–40, 42
        non-fungibility and, 36
        password-protected tools, 45
        property derivatives, 44
        single stock futures, 48
        small and mid-cap companies, 40
    competition and trading decisions
        capitalism and, 22
        commodity business, 31
        consolidation, reasons for, 23
        critical components, 30
        customer needs and, 30
        ECN platforms, 31
        equities business, 21–22, 25
        floor brokers, 32
        internalization business, 26–27
        liquidity pool, 26
        options business, 25
        order-flow competition, 27
        Reg NMS and, 23, 25–29
        share growth, calculation, 29
Intra-Day Cross, block crossing network, 32
ITG's DarkServer, 73

K

Ketchum, R., 97
Kinney, C., 89–97
Kloess, S., 8, 16–17
Krell, D., 21–22, 25, 27, 35–36

L

Labuszewski, J., 40, 41, 44, 48, 51
Lead market maker (LMM), 38
Lipper Large-Cap Value Funds Index, 76
Liquidity trading
    algorithms and technology products in, 56
    alternative sources of, 53
    DarkServer algorithm in, 64
    ECN aggregation in, 57
    input parameters for, 63
    Instinet's crossing system, 54
    institutional and retail investors, 58
    models competing in, 60
    non-displayed pools of, 61
    predatory algorithms, growth of, 54
    retail and wholesale markets in, 64
    routing engines in, 67
    shares and stocks of, 59
    stock markets for, 58
    transaction research
        in crossing and portfolio
            management, 55
Liquidnet, trading systems, 24
London's Big Bang in October 1986, 100
London Stock Exchange, 12, 57, 97

M

Mahoney, T., 72
Malta Stock Exchange, 10
Markets in Financial Instruments Directive
    (MiFID), 57–59
    consolidation and, 9
    data availability, 15
    internalization and, 2
    Reg ATS rules, 19
    trade reporting, 13
MatchPoint Trading, 74
McCreevy, C., 17
McGonegal, J., 40, 44, 49–50
MDAX stocks, 105
Merrill, L., 75
Merrill's program desk, 61
Mid-cap stocks, 80
Money show and intermarket competition, 47
Murphy, M., 69, 70

N

NASDAQ Stock Market, 23, 25–27, 30–32,
    34, 59, 65, 66, 94, 96–98. *See also*
    Stock Exchange Market
    Global Select Market, 46
    listings competition business

        performance and price perspective, 39
        visibility and, 39–40
    NYSE listed stocks and, 28–29
    online, electronic platform, 39
    under-covered companies, 42
National market system, 14
New York Stock Exchange (NYSE), 59, 67,
    68, 89, 90, 93–95, 97. *See also*
        Stock Exchange Market
    architecture, fast and slow component, 102
    crossing networks in, 68
    first trade and, 21
    floor-based system, 100
    Hybrid Market and, 103–104
    and hybrid system, 72
    listings business, 38
    Rule 390 and, 72
    value proposition, components, 38

O

O'Brien, W., 39, 42, 46–47, 49–50, 52
Off-exchange trading, 103
OMX AB, Swiss-Finnish financial services
    company, 10
On-book trading in Germany, 104
OneChicago, single stock futures, 48
Options Clearing Corp. (OCC), 35
OTC markets, 5

P

Pagano, M., 7–11, 14–20
Perfumo, D., 5
Pipeline, trading systems, 24, 32
Pisani, B., 21–36
Plexus Average Execution Gain/Loss
    of ITG, 79
Price discovery, 101

Q

Quantity discovery, 101

R

Reck, M., 7, 13–14, 17–18
Reg NMS Rule 605, 39
Ross, J., 53, 54, 56, 61

S

Schwartz, R. A., 8–10, 17, 89–92, 94–98
SDAX stocks, 105

Selway, J., 37–38, 40–42, 44–46, 48–49, 51–52
SETS trading system, 32
SIGMA X smart router, 54, 60, 61, 64
  in GSEC, 60
Society of American Business Editors and Writers, 89
Sofianos, G., 53, 54, 60, 65, 74
SpotFX, 5
Stock Exchange Market
  broker-dealer market, 90
  brokers and traders, 74
  buy-side and sell-side, 72
  dialogs between Schwartz, R. A. and Francioni, R.
    brokers and exchanges, 4–5
    consolidation, key drivers of, 1
    cost synergies, 4
    merger, assessment, 1–2
    netting, 2–3
    price discovery, 3
  e-quotes, 93–94
  governance, trading structure and strategy in, 96
  hybrid market
    arca and, 95–96
    auction, 89, 91
    in Europe, 90
    exchange traded funds, 94
    New York Stock Exchange (NYSE), 89–90, 94
    opening and closing procedures in, 95
  liquidity, 73, 75
  liquidity in, 90, 91
  outsourcing and, 87

  post-trade clearing and settlement, 17
  and regulations of rates, 69
  technology in
    animation, 91
  transparency and, 75
Stuchfield, N., 8, 9, 11, 13, 15–18, 20, 29, 90

T
Tabb, L, 53, 55, 56, 63, 66, 67
TECDAX technology stocks, 105
Thain, J., 22, 24
TIAA-CREF, 4
Tokyo Stock Exchange
  growth potential and, 9
Toronto stock exchange, 49–50
Transaction Cost Analysis, 79
Tudor Investments, 71

V
VWAP trading system on Wall Street, 73

W
Wood, R., 20
The World is Flat, 72
Wright, M., 53, 54, 57, 64, 76

X
Xetra Best-platform and internalization, 2
Xetra on-book order, 104
Xontro, Exchange's electronic order routing system, 104

Printed in the United States of America